DYING ROSE

DYING ROSE

| Douglas | Kathryn | Emily | Gemma |
| SMITH | BERMINGHAM | OLLE | JONES |

HarperCollins*Publishers*

HarperCollins*Publishers*
Australia • Brazil • Canada • France • Germany • Holland • India
Italy • Japan • Mexico • New Zealand • Poland • Spain • Sweden
Switzerland • United Kingdom • United States of America

HarperCollins acknowledges the Traditional Custodians
of the lands upon which we live and work, and pays respect
to Elders past and present.

First published on Gadigal Country in Australia in 2025
by HarperCollins*Publishers* Australia Pty Limited
ABN 36 009 913 517
harpercollins.com.au

Copyright © Douglas Smith, Kathryn Bermingham, Emily Olle and Gemma Jones 2025

The right of Douglas Smith, Kathryn Bermingham, Emily Olle and Gemma Jones to be
identified as the authors of this work has been asserted by them in accordance with the *Copyright
Amendment (Moral Rights) Act 2000.*

This work is copyright. Apart from any use as permitted under the *Copyright Act 1968*, no part
may be reproduced, copied, scanned, stored in a retrieval system, recorded, or transmitted, in any
form or by any means, without the prior written permission of the publisher. Without limiting
the author's and publisher's exclusive rights, any unauthorised use of this publication to train
generative artificial intelligence (AI) technologies is expressly prohibited. HarperCollins also
exercise their rights under Article 4(3) of the Digital Single Market Directive 2019/790 and
expressly reserve this publication from the text and data mining exception.

A catalogue record for this book is available from the National Library of Australia

ISBN 978 1 4607 6656 9 (paperback)
ISBN 978 1 4607 1785 1 (ebook)
ISBN 978 1 4607 3918 1 (audiobook)

Cover design by Michelle Zaiter, HarperCollins Design Studio
Cover artwork courtesy of the *Advertiser* (Adelaide); cover photos courtesy of Courtney Hunter-
Hebberman (Rose Hunter-Hebberman); Alma Warrior (Charlene Warrior); Dijana Damjanovic
(Lasonya Dutton); Susan Nowland (Lyla Nettle); Lena-Rose Campbell (Shanarra Bright
Campbell); Sharon Moore (Charli Powell)
Typeset in Bembo MT Pro by Kirby Jones

Printed and bound in the United States

Aboriginal and Torres Strait Islander readers are advised that this book contains the names and images of people who have died, used with the permission of their families.

REACH OUT FOR HELP

- In an emergency, call **000**
- Aboriginal and Torres Strait Islander people requiring crisis support can call
  13YARN (13 92 76)
- Anyone needing help with issues of mental health or depression can call
  Lifeline on 13 11 14 or Beyond Blue on 1300 224 636
- If you or someone you know is experiencing sexual abuse or family violence, call
  1800RESPECT (1800 737 732)
- Men experiencing anger or relationship issues can call
  Men's Referral Service on 1300 766 491

CONTENTS

Authors' note • ix

How It Began • xi
Rose Hunter-Hebberman • 3
Charlene Warrior • 47
Lasonya Dutton • 95
Lyla Nettle • 137
Shanarra Bright Campbell • 203
Charli Powell • 227
Dying to be Heard • 269

Acknowledgements • 295

AUTHORS' NOTE

While the media generally avoids reporting details about suicide, to understand the families' concerns about these cases it is important to give the full context of these tragic deaths. These details have been included at the families' request.

HOW IT BEGAN

'If you think it's hard being a white woman in Australia,' Courtney Hunter-Hebberman said, 'try being a black woman.'

The clattering of chairs and clinking of glasses stopped, and the marquee fell silent. Hundreds of guests at long tables swung around to see Courtney, up on the stage at the lectern.

Until she said those words, her Welcome to Country had been everything you would expect. She had acknowledged Elders, her language, her culture and how First Nations people care for the land. It was all very familiar. Then, because it was International Women's Day, she had turned to the subject of how First Nations women are treated.

All anyone could hear was birds chirping in the tall gumtrees outside.

Courtney's final words came in a rush.

'My daughter died and I've had no justice. She was only nineteen.'

Her shoulders slumped, and as she left the stage she looked forlorn.

The crowd was still silent at first, then a murmur rose.

Who was this woman who had just bared her soul? And who was her daughter, the girl who had died so young?

Then the afternoon carried on: lunch was served; a motivational speaker took to the stage; a local radio host said and did all the things expected of a compere at a corporate event.

By the time the formalities finished, Courtney was long gone. Her work done, she'd headed home, unaware of the buzz her words had created.

* * *

Gemma Jones, editor of the *Advertiser* in Adelaide, was a guest at the lunch that day. When the speakers had all left the stage, she went around the marquee trying to find Courtney, and then, when she couldn't, she found the event's host and asked for Courtney's number. After hearing her speak, Gemma wanted to know more.

When they talked, Courtney was friendly and warm – if a bit surprised by Gemma's interest. She said later she couldn't believe someone had listened to her and wanted to hear her daughter's story.

They arranged to meet, and a few weeks later Gemma and Kathryn Bermingham, the *Advertiser's* state political editor, were on their way to visit Courtney at her home in

How It Began

Campbelltown, a quiet, reasonably well-to-do Adelaide suburb not far from the city. Kathryn had recently reported on the death of another young First Nations woman, and Gemma saw parallels between that story and what Courtney had told her about Rose.

Courtney met them at her door and ushered them down a long hallway into a bright, open kitchen and living room. It was quite obviously a happy family home. A pet dog greeted them, a kitten stretched out in a nearby basket, and young boys were milling around making after-school snacks.

But something about the room struck them.

The presence of Courtney's daughter, Rose, was palpable.

In one corner was a bookshelf stacked with Rose's belongings and adorned with photos, trinkets, flowers and fairy lights, like a shrine. On the top shelf was a beautiful professional photo of Rose, printed on canvas. She looked barely nineteen, and so happy she glowed. A smile spread across her face, and her warm brown eyes, so like her mother's, were staring straight at the camera. A cherubic young boy was on her shoulders, hands in front of his face as if he was playing peekaboo.

On the lounge nearby sat Courtney's mother, Mandy Brown, there to support her daughter and share her own memories of Rose.

Courtney retrieved boxes from a cupboard, containing all that was left of her daughter's life. There were receipts,

xiii

scraps of paper, handwritten notes – snippets of Rose's final months – along with her old phone, autopsy notes and a few other bits and pieces Courtney had kept in the hope they would all be examined by police one day.

Then the words came tumbling out. Grief, she said, hit like a train at times, but she could talk about her daughter's death now without crying.

Rose had died just over two years ago, Courtney said, in December 2019. She was found slumped on a lounge in a tiny shed at the rear of the property she was living in. The police said it was suicide. This had come as a huge shock to the family, and they weren't convinced, Courtney said – but when they'd tried to ask questions, they felt like no one was listening.

With the family's permission, we formed a team to investigate Rose's death. There were four of us: Gemma and Kathryn were joined by senior reporter Emily Olle, whose background in television meant she knew audio, and Douglas Smith, who joined the *Advertiser* as Indigenous affairs reporter just as we began our research. Our plan was to produce a podcast, to make people listen. We would ask the questions Courtney craved answers for.

We started with the death of one young Indigenous woman. We could never have known that within months we would be examining five more.

* * *

How It Began

At first we were focused exclusively on Rose Hunter-Hebberman's story, and we named the podcast for her: *Dying Rose*. The scope of the project expanded rapidly, though, as we learned about other young women who had died in similar circumstances. The same sequence of events played out with heartbreaking regularity: while we were investigating one woman's story, we would uncover another. Courtney led us to some of these stories, and Douglas to others.

In each of the cases we investigated, a young woman had died suddenly and unexpectedly, and her death had been ruled a suicide, leaving her family struggling to understand, confounded by their grief.

These young women were all daughters, all sisters. Some were young mothers.

All were let down in a multitude of ways before and after they died, but almost no one seemed to have noticed.

You will come to know their names in these pages: not just Rose, but also Charlene, Lasonya, Lyla, Shanarra and Charli.

* * *

We started by travelling the country, tape recorders in tow, interviewing the women's families. Emily joined Kathryn on regular visits to Rose's mother Courtney in Adelaide, each visit leaving them with more leads to chase up. Doug spent hours with Charlene's family, recording her parents and brothers and sisters.

One after another, the families told us almost the same story. Only the details of how their daughters had died were different.

Charlene Warrior vanished from the blink-and-you'd-miss-it service town of Bute, South Australia. She'd gone there to pick up her baby daughter and hadn't returned. Charlene's desperate sister told police she would never just disappear like that, but it was more than a week before they started their search for her.

Lasonya Dutton's uncle discovered her decomposing body in the backyard of the family home in Wilcannia, in outback New South Wales. Police told the family her body had been lying there, just outside the kitchen window, for days – yet none of them had seen it.

Lyla Nettle was discovered in a dusty creek bed at Bolivar, north of Adelaide. Even the police acknowledge that the location and position of her body were unusual. Lyla's mother doesn't understand why they say her death was a suicide, because the pathologist's report didn't rule out the involvement of another person.

Shanarra Bright-Campbell attempted suicide in the backyard of her mother's flat in Alice Springs. When the police arrived, her brother was distraught: they needed an ambulance, he said, not police. He was arrested and dragged from the house as his mother shouted that her daughter was dying and needed help.

xvi

How It Began

And Charli Powell was only seventeen when she was found dead in the men's toilet block at a sports field in Queanbeyan, just south of Canberra. Her family feel that the police failed to ask even the most basic questions about how Charli came to be in the toilet block and what had happened to her.

One way or another, the families all said the same thing: they felt the police had been too quick to judge. 'Aboriginal, mental health issues, young woman, must be suicide.'

Only Shanarra's family accept that verdict without any question. The other women's families remain uncertain – and even in Shanarra's case, her mother wonders if her daughter could have been saved, had the police responded differently.

The families all felt that authorities hadn't taken their concerns seriously. In their view, police had failed to properly investigate their loved ones' deaths or consider crucial evidence.

We were struck every time by the painful questions they'd been left with.

Questions about how their loved ones had died. About what had really happened, and who was responsible. About the progress of police investigations.

They wanted to know more, to understand. They wanted proof. But no one would answer their questions, they said. No one was listening.

'Why will no one listen to us?'

They asked this question over and over.

* * *

In the course of our investigation, we spoke to witnesses and officials, although it was frustratingly difficult to find anyone in authority willing or able to consent to be interviewed.

At the same time, we gathered all the available evidence we could.

Early on, we collected postmortem reports. Their language was cold and clinical, without any emotion, yet they provoked so much heartache. Here were young women undergoing autopsies that showed them to have been in perfect physical health prior to their deaths, each reduced now to a list of body parts, all carefully weighed and measured by pathologists who had examined them from head to foot to determine an official cause of death. The physical detail was sometimes distressing, even horrifying.

We spent nearly eighteen months combing through it all, poring over police reports and the interviews we'd done, looking for leads, trying to understand how these women came to die. For much of this time, we were sequestered in an audio recording room, away from the noise and bustle of the *Advertiser*'s busy newsroom. At the end of each week, we'd meet to brief each other on developments. The mood was

How It Began

usually sombre, and at times we would be rendered speechless by what the others had learned.

The stories we uncovered were shocking – but what we found particularly disturbing, as reporters, was the lack of attention they'd received. These woman had died in circumstances that were hard to fathom, yet their stories hadn't received wall-to-wall media coverage. Their deaths weren't seen as out of the ordinary enough to interest the public or play on its sympathies. To the women's grieving families, it seemed, understandably, that no one really cared.

But for Douglas this was not surprising. He knew the world the women had lived and died in – a world in which disadvantage and indifference are inseparably entwined.

* * *

Douglas belongs to the Kokatha nation, whose traditional lands span much of South Australia's harsh, dry centre, and the Mirning nation, the whale dreaming people whose country stretches from the ancient seabed of the Nullarbor Plain down to the Great Australian Bight.

His grandparents were both born in scrub, in the red dirt. His grandmother, Mary Harrison, was born behind a football oval, with aunties attending the happy arrival, while his grandfather, Archie Barton, was born at a railway siding. Archie was a member of the Stolen Generations, the 'half-caste' child of a white father who was forcibly taken from his mother at age four or five and sent to the mission at Port Augusta, hundreds of kilometres away. Barton wasn't his real name; it was the name of the station he embarked from on his way to the mission. He never saw his mother again.

Archie Barton grew up to be the famous activist and Maralinga land custodian who, in the early 1990s, took soil laced with plutonium to London and, during a meeting with a parliamentary under-secretary, put it under the man's desk. Barton was there to appeal to the British to clean up his people's land, poisoned by nuclear testing in the 1950s and early 1960s. The under-secretary got a shock when Barton told him to look under his desk. Radiation from the tests was ruining the health of the Maralinga Tjarutja people, and Barton thought it was only fair that the under-secretary get a taste of their fears. Barton's activism, like that of so many First Nations activists, was forged by urgent need and a powerful desire for justice, and it still resonates with his journalist grandson today.

Douglas's father and Charlene Warrior's were brother boys: though Douglas's father grew up on the Nullarbor Plain and Charlene's father in Adelaide and on the Point Pearce mission on the Yorke Peninsula, they'd known each other as kids.

Douglas himself was born in Port Lincoln on the Eyre Peninsula, a tough place, and had a difficult start, almost dying in his first few days of life. He was left at the hospital for eight weeks before his aunty asked his father if she could pick him

How It Began

up and keep him. In his culture, aunties are called mothers, and Mum Theresa took baby Douglas home. Tragically, she died when he was about eighteen months old.

Douglas says he has been to more funerals than he can remember. His aunt's funeral was just one of many he has attended over the course of his life. 'There's funerals all the time,' he says. 'Sometimes it is violence, but a lot of the time it is sickness – bad health, people dying at early ages. And now they're dying a lot younger than usual. A lot of cousins of mine. Drinking, drugs, car accidents, suicide.'

When his aunty died, his grandparents took him into their care. He says Archie and Mary grew him up as 'Mum' and 'Dad' in Ceduna on South Australia's west coast. He always had three dads growing up: Archie; Mum Theresa's partner, Alan; and his biological father, Mary's son Steven.

Douglas first hunted goanna at age seven, at a place called Emu, north of Maralinga Village. He did an interview in front of TV cameras for the first time on the same day.

The Maralinga Lands are his homelands. Growing up with Mary and Archie, he went out camping regularly. They would sometimes spend two weeks out bush around the Gawler Ranges, or along the Nullarbor Coast, with his older sister Danielle and his brother-in-law, Roger. He says hunting and camping were pretty much a part of life for him growing up, the best times of his life. His grandparents took him everywhere and taught him everything about the bush. 'I

xxi

could sing any song of Slim Dusty from a young age,' he says, 'as that's all we listened to.'

Douglas had his first encounter with the police at age ten: he was with a group of kids, and one of them – not Douglas – shouted something cheeky but harmless, like 'hey' or 'oi', at a police car driving by. The car stopped and an officer got out, walked straight up to him and threatened to arrest him. As he grew up, he was often stopped on the street by the police and questioned for no reason, especially when he was with other Indigenous kids. Having to give officers his details and, in some cases, being searched and questioned about things he knew nothing about, was traumatising. 'Police are usually the last line of call for Aboriginal people if we're ever in trouble,' he says, 'because we've never really been treated fairly.'

When he was about fourteen, Douglas moved to Adelaide. Others in the house were using drugs, and he routinely stole food to get by. 'When you're living in that environment, when you've only got rice in the cupboard, you'll do anything to get food, anything. I had to steal food from shops. You steal to eat,' he said.

'When I was a young fella I spent a week in a youth training centre. They didn't have anywhere to send me – no family wanted me back. There was no one to come and get me.' It was a difficult time in his life. The seminal moment in Douglas's youth came soon after, when at the age of fifteen he attempted suicide in the backyard. He was unconscious, his

xxii

How It Began

life slipping away, when a cousin burst into the yard and saved him. From that moment he vowed to embrace all that life had to offer and to succeed.

'Something saved my life,' Douglas says. 'I went and stayed with my Christian family, Alan's mum and dad. My nan, she sorted me out. My pop, he sorted me out.'

He was scouted to play AFL in the state league in Western Australia at fifteen, but injury cut short any dreams of a footy career only a few months later. He spent a formative year in his late teens at home around Ceduna and Oak Valley, absorbing his culture and hunting, before going to work full-time.

Douglas had several different jobs over the years, spending time as an oyster farmer, a firefighter and a mechanic. It was while he was living in Victoria, working in forestry and as a firefighter, that he learned he could do a bridging course to overcome not finishing school and get into university.

His uncle said, 'You should go to university. The University of Adelaide is offering a bridging course,' Douglas recalls.

'We were out in the paddock planting trees, and I told my mates and they said, "You can't spell your own name."'

But he seized the opportunity. He'd had a burning desire to tell the stories of his people since he was a boy. Douglas completed the bridging course and was accepted into a journalism degree. He has not looked back.

* * *

Having Douglas on our team was critical to the success of the *Dying Rose* podcast. Our original idea was to investigate a young woman's death. It was thanks to Douglas's perspective and experience, and the generosity of the young women's families, that we were able to investigate an even bigger story.

Each of the young women's deaths that you will read about in this book was a tragedy for those who loved her. Together, they reveal a tragedy on a national scale, one that should have us all demanding answers.

ROSE HUNTER-HEBBERMAN

There were some odd sorts living in the housing block, of course, but most of the residents were just ordinary people, trying to get by in a world that had been far from kind. They kept to themselves, for the most part, and drew their curtains at any whiff of trouble. The block of units, while rough around the edges, was an unlikely crime scene.

But on 4 December 2019 – a typically warm, bright early summer's day in Adelaide – a teenage girl was found dead just a stone's throw from the back door of one of those units, in a backyard shed. She was seated on the ground, slumped against a mottled couch, one cheek resting on its rough fabric cover.

Rose Hunter-Hebberman was nineteen years old. She was tiny, with long brown hair that fell across her shoulders. She was wearing blue and white leggings and a grey t-shirt. Around her wrist was a black hair tie, and on her finger a white metal ring set with a light green stone. Above her left ankle was a tattoo – a red rose.

Tiny flecks of blood had dripped from her blue-green lips onto the couch cover.

A kelpie was huddled beside her. Around Rose's neck was a thin dog lead, no more than a few centimetres wide. At its end was a metal clasp. The lead looked hardly strong enough to withstand the force of a boisterous dog pulling at it, let alone the weight of a human body.

Above Rose's head, a few metal beams ran across the shed's width.

The shed was two metres across and four metres deep – hardly bigger than a large dining table.

This was where Rose's final moments had unfolded.

It was her friend, a young man we'll call Jared, who called the police. When they arrived, just after 4 pm, Jared was waiting for them in the house.

They found Rose's body outside in the shed.

The officers' conclusion, on the basis of their preliminary investigations, was simple. The cause of death was suicide.

Rose had hanged herself with the thin dog lead, they said. Eventually it had snapped under the weight of her delicate frame.

They did not know why she had hanged herself, but they believed that they knew how.

Her body was still slumped against the couch, exactly where they'd found it, as they noted their findings and waited for the coroner's van to arrive.

Rose Hunter-Hebberman

* * *

It was in March 2022 that the *Advertiser*'s editor, Gemma Jones, and state political editor, Kathryn Bermingham, first visited Courtney Hunter-Hebberman at her home in Adelaide's north-eastern suburbs. Gemma had heard Courtney make brief reference to Rose's story at an International Women's Day event and had tracked her down, wanting to know more.

Kathryn returned soon after, this time with senior reporter Emily Olle. Kathryn and Emily had never met before: Gemma had just hired Emily with this new project partly in mind, but Emily hadn't officially begun at the *Advertiser* when she and Kathryn first visited Courtney together. They brought with them a notepad, a voice recorder and a list of questions about Rose's final days and the years that followed.

Courtney's house sits on a medium-sized block in Campbelltown, a part of the city best known for its vibrant Italian community and hearty food. The unmistakeable sound of children playing greeted Kathryn and Emily through the flyscreen mesh as they knocked at the front door.

Courtney opened it, her long dark hair falling in waves over her shoulders. A young boy, about five or six, hovered by her side. She grinned as she welcomed Kathryn and Emily in.

The house was a modern build, but it was laid out like an old Victorian terrace with bedrooms dotting the sides of a long hallway. It was clearly home to a loving family: clothes and toys were strewn around, and framed photos covered almost every available part of the hallway walls. At the end of the hall was a bright, open kitchen and living area.

Sitting on the dark leather couch was Courtney's mother, Mandy Brown. Above her hung the crimson, black and gold of a large Aboriginal flag. Mandy had come along to support Courtney, just as she had when Gemma and Kathryn first visited. Mandy was the epitome of classic style, wearing a button-up blouse, her lips painted a rich burgundy. We would soon learn that she was the matriarch of the family, and Courtney's rock.

As Kathryn and Emily looked around, they saw Rose's belongings arranged on the wooden bookshelf in the corner, adorned with flowers and fairy lights, and atop this shrine Rose's portrait. The young woman in the photograph was extraordinarily attractive, with long brown hair, bright eyes and a brilliant smile.

They recognised the child on Rose's shoulders in the photo: it was the boy who'd been hovering at Courtney's side when she welcomed them in. He was Rose's nephew, Courtney explained. Her daughter had loved her family, she said, and was a favourite with her younger siblings and their cousins, especially the little ones, who delighted in her energy and sense of fun.

Rose was vivacious, Courtney said. 'A really bubbly, bright young girl. Really beautiful too. She loved to have her hair and makeup done, everything like that.'

Her daughter had been taught to be proud of her Peramangk and Ngarrindjeri heritage, she said. Rose came from a line of strong women and had grown up watching them speak up for what they believed in. She was fiercely independent and always 'did her own thing', but she also had a huge heart and was incredibly generous.

It was clear that for Rose's family, the pain and grief of her loss were still fresh.

Kathryn and Emily perched on the end of the couch. Emily set up their tape recorder, and when Courtney was ready, she hit record.

'Tell us about the day Rose died,' Kathryn said.

Courtney did. She explained that, on the morning of 4 December 2019, she was walking her younger kids to school when she got a phone call from Rose.

'She was quite upset and asked if I could come down and pick her up,' Courtney said.

Rose had spent the night at Jared's house in Black Forest, in the inner south of Adelaide, about half an hour's drive from Campbelltown. It's a leafy area, full of well-heeled families, but Jared's flat was in a Housing Trust block, designed to provide people on low incomes with affordable accommodation. Rose had met Jared through one of her brothers and had been spending time with him on and off for a few months.

Courtney said her daughter's relationship with Jared was tumultuous at best. They often had huge arguments, and Rose would walk out on Jared.

'They weren't really in a relationship, you know … They just kind of hung out together. Sometimes she stayed at his house and things like that,' Courtney said. 'Jared wasn't really good for her … They'd been sort of seeing each other for a bit, but that morning she was really, really upset,' Courtney said. 'She told me she wanted to leave.'

But Rose and Jared had a kelpie, Phoenix. Rose loved Phoenix 'more than anything', her mother said, and didn't want to leave him behind.

'She wanted to leave there, but she couldn't leave the dog.'

Courtney was feeling unwell that day – she had a migraine – but she offered to pick Rose up after she had dropped the other kids off at school. When Rose declined, Courtney suggested that she take Phoenix for a walk to try to clear her head.

Courtney sent her daughter a few more text messages that morning and then went back to bed because she was feeling so unwell.

Around 2 pm, Courtney woke up. She noticed that Rose hadn't replied to her messages, which was unusual for her, but she didn't think much of it, as Rose had been planning to meet her younger brother Liam for lunch.

Maybe she's just hanging out with Liam, Courtney thought.

'I was just sort of lying there on the couch, scrolling Facebook,' she said. Jared had posted that he was at work, though he usually worked the later shift.

'I can't remember exactly what it said, but I remember that I commented on it. I said, "Are you and Rose still fighting? Where's Phoenix and where is Rose?"

'But he never replied.'

Courtney fell back asleep. 'I was having really disturbing, dark dreams,' she said. She described seeing a demon figure, small and slight, surrounded by deep black and red. 'Our neighbours had a fire going the night before,' she said, and she'd thought maybe that had just 'carried over' into her subconscious. 'But I remember it so distinctly,' she said. 'I can still see it in my head.' She woke with the feeling that 'something wasn't right'.

At about 4 pm, after Courtney had picked the younger kids up from school, Liam called her. Rose had never turned up for lunch.

That worried Courtney. 'Rose always kept a date and always turned up on time,' she said.

Liam said he'd been trying to find her, calling her phone and sending her messages on Facebook, but Rose wasn't replying, and he didn't know where she was.

'That's when I knew in my gut something was really wrong,' Courtney said. 'I checked Facebook Messenger and saw that she hadn't been active. So I was like, "No, I'm gonna ring the police."

'I rang triple zero straightaway and told them my daughter was missing. They said, "Just wait twenty-four hours, she's probably off doing something.""*

It felt like they weren't taking the situation seriously, she said – as if they were trying to palm her off.

By then it was early evening and there was still no sign of Rose.

'I was starting to panic,' Courtney said, 'because for none of us to hear from her all day was really unusual.'

At around 6 pm, a car pulled up outside her house.

For the first time since starting her story, Courtney paused. She had a faraway look in her eyes, as if she were no longer in the room. She had been transported back to that moment – the moment her life changed forever.

'You know the sound of a cop car ... I've heard those doors a thousand times ... And it's not just one door, it's two doors. *Boom, boom.* Straightaway, I knew. I knew why they were there.

'I got up and went to the front door. It was a young male and a female. They asked, "Can we come in?" and I told them, "I already know why you're here.""

Courtney took a breath.

'We got halfway down the hallway, and all the kids were there. I was already crying by that stage, and then the young male cop was crying – he couldn't even say it.

---

* You do *not* have to wait twenty-four hours to report someone missing in Australia. If you have serious concerns for their safety and you don't know where they are, you should file a missing persons report at your local police station as soon as possible.

'The young female was still by the door, and the male had come in. He was shaking his head and he was crying. He just said, "I'm sorry, I'm sorry."

'That's when I just went into my kitchen, and I felt like my body was twisting sideways. It was like a blackout in my mind. My only thought was, *I want to go down there* – to where Rose was found. So I asked where she was. They said Jared's house, but then they told us no, that we actually couldn't go down there.'

Until the coroner's van had taken Rose's body away, the police couldn't let anyone onto the property.

'I was just sitting there,' she said. 'I didn't know what to do. I asked, "How did she die?"

'They told me she was found hanging.'

Courtney asked what Rose had been hanging from, and the police said she hadn't actually been found hanging. The narrow dog lead she'd used had snapped, they said, and her body had been found slumped against the couch below.

But Courtney didn't believe her daughter had tried to kill herself.

'She was leaving Jared's place that morning. She wanted to leave. That was what she was doing, right? She always says what she's going to do, you know, so I thought, *No way.*'

Besides, if Rose *had* decided to kill herself, Courtney was sure she'd have told her family. She'd have sent a message saying, 'I'm going to kill myself,' or 'I'm going to take my life.'

But Rose hadn't sent anything to anyone.

'To none of us,' Courtney said. 'Not to her older brother, not to her younger brother, not to my mum, not to me.

'Then, *boom*, all of a sudden, what? She's just dead?'

Tears welled in her eyes. Kathryn and Emily paused the recording, but Courtney was stoic, insisting that they go on. She hadn't finished telling her story.

* * *

When a body is found, it is usually taken to the morgue, where a family member or close friend is asked to formally identify it.

Courtney had believed that identifying Rose's body would be her job – a final act of love to farewell the little girl she had raised for nineteen years.

But by the time she learned where her daughter's body was being kept, it was too late.

'I rang up the hospital, because I didn't even know where they take bodies, you know?' Courtney said. 'I didn't know where she was going or what was happening.'

As Rose's 'domestic partner', Jared – not her mother – was considered Rose's next of kin, and the police had already asked him to formally identify her body.

He had been the one to close the book on Rose's story. Courtney was denied even that last small act of love.

'I had to beg to go and see her body in the coroner's office,' she said.

When she arrived at the morgue on 5 December 2019, she was guided through to the cold room.

'We weren't allowed to go near her, to touch her, because at that stage the person's body is classed as evidence of the state. It's like, *Well, that might be your evidence, but that's our family member.*'

Rose's body was draped in white sheets and surrounded by flowers, but what Courtney saw were the blue-green bruises all over her daughter's beautiful face. Rose had blood on her lips, and one of her teeth was missing.

Something's not right, Courtney thought.

'My head started to really tick,' she said.

Before Rose's death, Courtney had been studying law at the University of Adelaide, and one of the areas of law she found most interesting was evidence.

'I'm always thinking, thinking, thinking,' she said. 'Sometimes it does my head in because I think too much, but I was standing there that day telling myself, *Try not to be emotional. Just think.*'

* * *

When a young woman's body is discovered, questions should be raised.

How did she die? Could there have been foul play?

Statistics tell us there are a few likely answers. But what we need to understand is that those answers vary from community to community.

In 2022, the most recent year for which figures are available, suicide accounted for around 4.6 per cent of all deaths of First Nations people in Australia. The comparable rate for non-Indigenous Australians was 1.6 per cent, meaning that First Nations people are nearly three times more likely to die by suicide than other Australians.

Policing relies, in many ways, on assumptions about what is likely. Police officers assess a situation for danger and evaluate probable outcomes on the basis of their training and prior experience, and they interpret evidence in the same way. But police work also requires an open mind, because the most obvious conclusion may not be the correct one. Scepticism, many officers would attest, is a key component of good policing.

All of us have unconscious biases: beliefs, assumptions or attitudes that influence our thoughts and actions without us realising it. Unconscious biases are hard to fight because, by definition, we are not aware of them.

Sadly, it's not surprising that police officers might see the dead body of a young Indigenous person slumped against a couch in a shed and conclude that they had died by suicide: they know that suicide is the leading cause of death for young people in Australia, and they also know that the suicide rate is significantly higher among young First Nations people.

But in her daughter's case, Courtney Hunter-Hebberman found this conclusion surprising.

Rose was an usher at state government events and had been in her job for more than a year at that point. She loved the arts – she had worked in theatres and for an organisation called Country Arts SA, one of the state's biggest arts organisations – and she was booked to do some work at the Adelaide Fringe Festival. She already had savings in the bank, and she had just signed a contract to do some modelling. Courtney knew she was excited about her future.

'The police were trying to tell me Rose's death wasn't suspicious,' she said. 'But I'm thinking, *Bullshit. How's it not suspicious?*'

Next to her, Mandy nodded in silent agreement.

* * *

In December 2019, Rose's brother Liam had been living with Mandy, but he had stayed at Jared's house, not his grandmother's, the night before Rose died.

Mandy said it wasn't unusual for Liam to visit Rose at Jared's house, but it was the first time she had asked her brother to stay the night.

'I think she was scared and she wanted someone there,' she said.

When police asked to interview Liam on 5 December, the day after his sister was found dead, it was Mandy who took him to the police station.

'I voiced my concern over him being interviewed, because of his age,' Mandy told Kathryn and Emily. He was fourteen at the time.

Liam was told to come to the station at Christies Beach, almost an hour from where he lived.

'There was no offer of support, or even negotiation, or like, "Let's come to you,"' Mandy said. 'It was just, "You have to come down to Christies Beach."'

She felt the police showed no consideration, not stopping to think about what the family was going through. 'It felt cold and callous,' she said – especially when they were dealing with a young boy who had just lost his sister.

Mandy spoke to the woman who would be conducting the interview and asked if she could be present, as Liam's guardian. She felt her grandson needed someone there with him for support.

'Liam was really still in shock, so he couldn't respond to the officer as he normally would,' Mandy said. 'The line of questioning was like adult questioning, and he didn't understand it. There was no one there that was just offering him a conversation.'

Mandy didn't like the detective's 'procedural' approach, or her tone.

'She asked him what happened the night before. Liam said he heard Jared and Rose arguing. When he woke up to go to school the next day, he checked to make sure Rose was okay.

'He told the detective that Rose was sitting on the bed and she was upset. He said: "I asked her if she was okay, and she said yes. I told her I'd contact her later and we'd catch up, send me a text."

'And then he left. He told the detective he hadn't felt concerned about Rose.'

After the interview, Mandy asked to speak to the detective alone.

'She said to me, right then and there, that she was putting it down as suicide, which I was quite surprised about.

'She had already decided the outcome – without talking to me, without talking to other people, without me being allowed to voice my concerns. I just found it really odd that she was like: "Right, this is what it's going to be."'

Mandy said the detective tried to appeal to her, saying, 'I know you don't want it to be suicide,' as if she knew how Mandy felt but there was nothing she could do.

'Don't make that assumption,' Mandy told her. 'You don't know what I feel. If it was suicide, at least I know she had a choice. I don't believe she had a choice in this matter.'

'I told her that all I wanted was the truth,' Mandy said, 'whatever that was – because none of this was adding up.' But to her it seemed the police were 'just ticking the boxes', more interested in closure than truth, eager to be done with the case as quickly as possible.

To Mandy Brown – a member of the Stolen Generations, separated from her birth mother and culture as a child – their apparent lack of empathy was shameful in this day and age, reminding her of an earlier time.

It struck her as archaic, she said, to show so little regard for the loss of a human life.

* * *

Later that day, after the police interview, Mandy and Courtney went to Jared's house to see the place where Rose had died for the first time.

'We went to see where her body was and to look at the shed, you know … to make sure her spirit was moved on from that area,' Courtney said.

When they arrived, Jared was there with his mother. Courtney tried to hug him, but he was too tense. He was just standing there, she said – 'not crying, not doing anything'. Tension and grief hung in the air.

There was a Christmas tree in the corner of the living room – a cruel reminder of the holiday the family would soon spend without Rose. Jared and his mother sat by the Christmas tree, on the lounge.

Jared's mother just looked at them, Mandy said, not offering them anything.

Courtney walked outside to the shed where her daughter's body was found, followed cautiously by Rose's kelpie, Phoenix, who had been at the house with Jared overnight.

When she opened the shed door and saw the couch, her body crumpled. She fell onto it and clutched at the rough, blood-flecked fabric of its cover.

Jared had followed behind her. He stood on the grass and watched the scene unfold.

After a moment, Courtney lifted herself from the couch and looked around her, taking in the four-by-two shed in which her daughter had died.

Her analytical mind began ticking.

'I'm looking at the shed and I'm thinking, *Hang on a minute here. Where was she hanging from?*' Courtney said.

'There's dust, like really thick dust, on everything. That's the first thing I noticed.'

She stood up on the couch to examine the beams overhead. *She's had to climb up here to clip*, Courtney thought.

There were only a few beams. It should have been obvious which of them Rose had hanged herself from.

'But none of that dust was disturbed,' Courtney said.

* * *

Courtney wanted the police to keep investigating her daughter's death. She wasn't convinced that they had asked the right questions or spoken to the right people.

Everyone told her to let the authorities do their job, but she didn't trust them.

She didn't trust that her family would be treated in the same way as a non-Indigenous family.

'I've seen what they do with blackfellas and how they treat our people,' she said. 'In Australia, it's like there are two different groups. There's a racial bias that exists within our systems. It's not just in our heads as black people.

'That racial bias is embedded in the investigative process. We can't trust the police to investigate and actually reach an outcome. For us, there's no closure.'

She would have to be her own investigator, she decided, and find the answers for herself.

In the weeks that followed Rose's death, Courtney went back to the house – searching, in her own words, for 'other evidence'.

She had spoken with Jared about what to do with Rose's possessions, and he'd said she could take them all. The only thing he wanted to keep was her black scarf.

Courtney was determined to look in every cupboard and go through every single drawer in the house. She was looking for something – anything – that might help to ease her racing mind.

During one of her visits, she took the couch from the shed where Rose had died. To this day, that couch remains in storage.

On another visit, she went upstairs to the bedroom that Rose and Jared had shared, planning to go through Rose's drawers, pack her things and then look around to see what else she could find. She was shocked by the state of the room.

It was trashed, she said. 'Behind the bed, on the wall, there was blood and spit.' There were holes in the wall, too.

She couldn't make sense of it. 'Rose was an immaculate person, right? Everything had to be clean, everything had a place,' Courtney said.

She examined the holes in the wall, wondering how they got there and how recent they were, and then started looking around.

'In the bedroom there was a big TV cabinet. I kept feeling like something was saying to me, "Just keep looking, Mum," so I got in right behind there.'

There was another hole in the wall, a smaller one, behind the cabinet. Courtney discovered an old Nokia phone stuffed inside it.

That phone, Courtney believed, belonged to Jared. When she switched it on, the battery was nearly flat.

She opened up the notes app.

'He had all these little notes,' Courtney said. She found these notes disturbing, describing them as 'crazy'. Later, she said the language Jared used in them was violent.

'Then I looked in the contact list ... He had my daughter under "Dying Rose".'

Courtney pocketed the phone, believing it could help her understand her daughter's final moments.

She didn't know it then, but that had been the battery's final gasp. It would be more than four years before she was able to switch that phone on again.

She then started rummaging through a chest of drawers in the cupboard, where she found Rose's black scarf, neatly folded. She had given the scarf to Rose herself, one day when they had gone shopping together in the city.

'So I pulled it out,' Courtney said.

She had already told us that Rose took incredible pride in her appearance – 'If you knew Rose, you knew that she would never have a hair out of place' – and that her daughter had always taken good care of her belongings.

But when Courtney unfolded the scarf, it was filthy.

'It had saliva and snot all over it,' she said.

'Jared hadn't cried, hadn't shown any emotion whatsoever. So I thought, *No, I'm going to take this.* I always thought it was so unusual that he wanted to keep that scarf.'

Courtney paused. 'Oh god, I feel sick.'

For the first time during the almost two-hour interview, she was overcome by her emotions.

* * *

During the interview, both Courtney and Mandy returned more than once to a question that had not, at that point, been answered to their satisfaction. Where had Jared been when Rose died?

Jared worked at a bar in one of Adelaide's beachside suburbs. He usually worked the late shift and took public transport to get there. He had told police he'd worked the earlier shift that day and was at work when Rose had allegedly taken her life.

But, at least as far as Courtney and Mandy knew, police had never actually checked for CCTV footage that would prove Jared was at work and not with Rose when she died.

'If he'd gone to work,' Mandy said she asked police, 'why haven't you got the CCTV off the tram to show where he was and when he was coming to and from the flat? Or why aren't you questioning his boss further?'

The family had so many questions they wanted answered.

'Why aren't these questions being put to people?' Mandy asked one officer. 'Why aren't they being answered?'

'But they just dismissed my concerns,' she said.

One thing became clear to Kathryn and Emily early on — right from the start, even, at that very first interview. If police had checked for CCTV footage of Jared on the day Rose died, they hadn't told Courtney or Mandy.

If that footage existed, and if the police had watched it, seen Jared on the tram, *and then told Rose's family*, Courtney wouldn't have been sitting there that day in her living room with two journalists beside her on the couch. That footage – that single, undeniable piece of evidence – would have been enough to dispel all doubt, sparing Rose's family years of heartache.

There is nothing to suggest Jared wasn't at work that day when he said he was. In fact, as we will discuss, Courtney would later discover text messages that showed he *was* at work.

But back in March 2022, when we first met her, she'd had no confirmation either way. As far as Courtney knew, the police had never bothered to look for proof supporting Jared's claim.

'Where's the evidence that they went and checked if he was at work? Shouldn't that be recorded?' she said. 'I want to see that evidence. Maybe they did go down there, but we don't know about it.

'All we wanted was to feel like the police had investigated properly. Everything that we've said to them, all of our concerns, they should be investigated, right?'

She said the police just went: 'Aboriginal woman, mental health, fight with the boyfriend, topped herself, right?'

They probably made that assumption from the moment Jared called in Rose's death, Courtney said – as soon as he told them that she was Aboriginal, that was their conclusion.

They seemed to think it was that simple.

But Rose's family weren't so sure. They saw things the police didn't, other possibilities that should have been considered.

'As an Aboriginal family going to the police, it felt like they didn't look at all the evidence that we were trying to offer.

'Because it's not just about evidence in the eyes of the law,' Courtney said. 'There's all this other stuff, cultural stuff, that you need to think about to help put it all into context.'

The family wanted to help the police to understand, to put things in their proper context, but they felt their concerns were dismissed.

'This whole time we've been pushing, pushing, pushing ... telling them it needs to be investigated, it needs to be investigated.' Courtney choked back a sob. 'They never even listened to anything that we said. They never even checked if he was at work, you know. That's all we asked ... Just check that he was at work.'

Mandy felt the same: they hadn't been listened to, she said, and the police hadn't offered enough support.

'We didn't have an Aboriginal liaison officer, nothing,' she said. 'Nobody to debrief with, nobody to lean on. I spoke to officers multiple times about my concerns. Nothing.'

* * *

After several hours, Kathryn and Emily brought their first interview with Rose Hunter-Hebberman's family to an end. As they left, they gave both mother and grandmother a tight hug. The extraordinary trust Courtney and Mandy had shown in these two strangers, sharing Rose's story with them, made the reporters feel they were saying goodbye to friends.

They were determined to repay that trust.

The police investigation had left the family with questions about Rose's death, trapping them in their grief – but the *Dying Rose* reporting team would do everything it could to find answers for them.

* * *

A few weeks after that first interview, Courtney took Kathryn to the block of Housing Trust units where Rose died. Kathryn assumed they would take a look at the outside of the building and be on their way.

As they got out of the car, they saw neighbours drawing their blinds shut.

'This is it,' Courtney said.

'When was the last time you were here?' Kathryn asked.

'Oh my god … three years ago, I was just thinking that. I'm surprised I'm not having a panic attack and calling an ambulance,' Courtney said. 'I can't believe I'm coping.'

The long row of adjoined brick units was quiet.

Courtney pointed. 'That's the house, the second one.' Jared no longer lived there – he hadn't for some time.

It looked different now, Courtney said – the new resident clearly took more pride in their home than Jared ever had.

There was a well-kept front garden with planter boxes, a table and chairs. Courtney pointed out the window of the room where Rose had slept the night before she died.

When she knocked on the door, a slight woman cautiously opened it.

'Yes?'

Courtney introduced herself.

'Hello, I'm so sorry to disturb you. My name's Courtney, and this is Kathryn. I don't know how long you've lived here, but in 2019 my daughter died in the shed out the back.'

The woman quickly told Courtney she didn't actually live in the house. She was just a neighbour who was house-sitting. Kathryn thought she was going to slam the door on them – until she smiled at Courtney with obvious compassion.

The neighbour, whom we'll call Amy, said she lived a few doors down. She had been there for several years – and she'd known Rose.

Amy seemed sympathetic, and she invited them around the back of the house, so they could see the shed where Rose had died.

'Look at the chickens!' Courtney said excitedly as they walked across the grass, gesturing to a new coop built in the corner of the neat backyard. 'Rose would have loved them.'

Looking around her, Kathryn found it hard to believe something so awful had happened here.

Courtney showed them the shed.

'The couch was here,' she said.

There were only a few beams above their heads, but Courtney said police had not been able to tell her which one Rose had been hanging from.

It was a simple question – *Where did she hang from?* – and it should have had a simple answer.

But that one simple question was not answered on the day Rose died. When the police investigators packed up their kits that night and the coroner's van had arrived to remove Rose's body, that question remained unanswered.

Later, when Courtney had asked the police about it directly, they told her they might never know where Rose was hanging from before she fell.

'It really didn't add up,' Courtney said. 'In that little tiny space, how could they not tell where she was hanging?

'I'm looking at the shed and thinking, *How big is it? Two by four?*'

As Courtney surveyed her surroundings, Amy and Kathryn stepped back out into the garden. Amy told Kathryn that she and Rose had had a strange relationship: they used to walk their dogs together, always in comfortable silence.

'It was my first time living in a Housing Trust community,' Amy said, 'and I was a bit worried. I kept to myself to begin with … but I very quickly realised that it was a beautiful community, especially the oldies.

'I feel like I've made friends here. It's a little community of good people who look out for each other.

'I used to see this little black puppy walking across our front yard,' Amy said as Courtney rejoined them, 'and my dog would always bark at it.'

Both Courtney and Kathryn smiled, realising the black puppy was Rose's beloved kelpie, Phoenix.

'We met one time when I walked out the house and saw Rose and was like, "Hey, girl!"' Amy gave the greeting a Los Angeles lilt.

'Rose literally said, "Hey girl!" in the same accent, and we just walked around the block. And that was it.

'We ended up meeting each other out there at the same time once a week. I could tell that something wasn't right with her, but I never pressured her to talk about anything.

'The last time I saw her, it would have been about a week before she passed away. We were walking around the block, and she said to me …' Amy became visibly emotional, pausing to gather her breath.

'She said to me, "I wish us women had more strength, because even in our own homes we don't have the final say."

'That was the last thing she said to me.'

Kathryn asked Amy if she could go upstairs, to see the bedroom where Rose had slept the night before she died.

Amy happily obliged, leading her in the back door and up the stairs.

'What do you remember about the day Rose died?' Kathryn asked her. As she looked around, she noted that there were no holes in the walls. The holes must have been fixed and the walls painted. The bedroom was dated – like the house – but it was neat and tidy. It felt like a home.

'I remember it was my daughter's kindy day,' Amy replied. 'At about 7.30 I went outside to put my rubbish in the bin out the front and heard an argument. I saw him first ... He was waving his arms around and talking to her.'

Amy wiped away a tear. She said she'd heard them arguing for days and days, and him asking her to leave. 'That day, they were just yelling and screaming. I remember turning up the TV because I didn't want my daughter to hear any of what was happening. I couldn't hear what he was saying, but she was screaming, "Just go, just stop fucking doing this." I thought about going over there, but I didn't do it. I just remember coming back from picking my daughter up from kindy later that day and seeing not a big ambulance, but four of those little ambulances.

'The next thing I saw, there was a police paddy wagon.'

It turned out Amy hadn't known how that day had ended. 'We knew nothing about it at all until you rocked up here,' she said later.

According to Amy, police had never asked to interview

any of the neighbours after Rose's death. When she found out what had happened, she thought that was strange.

'Why didn't any police come and talk to us?' she said. 'Especially knowing that in these communities people talk and people are nosy. Someone might have known something.'

* * *

The second time Kathryn and Emily interviewed Courtney and Mandy, it was at the *Advertiser*'s offices in the Adelaide CBD.

It was four months after they had first met – and the reporters had just read Rose's autopsy report.

Rose's autopsy was conducted two days after her death, on 6 December 2019. But it had been months before Courtney received the full report.

Until that point, she had learned little about what police believed happened to her daughter, except that they believed her death to be suicide.

When the report finally arrived, it was, as all autopsy reports are, clinical and procedural. They have a set format: the examining pathologist provides brief notes on the deceased person's background and then summarises the findings of the postmortem autopsy before stating the officially determined cause of death.

Courtney opened the first page of the report.

DYING ROSE

BACKGROUND

The deceased was a 19-year-old female who was thought to suffer with mental health difficulties, for which she had been prescribed mirtazapine. She had apparently previously threatened self-harm.

The deceased was staying at a male's address and on the morning of 4/12/2019 when the man got up for work as a chef they argued verbally.

The man left for work and they exchanged text messages, including [one from] the deceased threatening to take his money and their pet dog.

The final paragraph of the background summary read:

He returned home and went outside into the shed, noticed the deceased's dog upon its bed with the deceased slumped against a couch with something around her neck.

He called an ambulance and loosened the ligature around her neck. Ambulance officers arrived and life was pronounced extinct. Police officers attended and noted the long end of the ligature hanging down the deceased's back. No suspicious circumstances were reported.

The pathologist summarised his findings on the final page:

Rose Hunter-Hebberman

SUMMARY OF MAJOR PATHOLOGICAL FINDINGS

1. Ligature constructed from dog lead in situ around the neck.
2. Corresponding rising ligature mark around neck.
3. Fine abrasions/superficial incisions inner-left wrist and forearm.
4. Congestion and petechial haemorrhages above the level of the ligature mark.
5. Pulmonary congestion.
6. Cannabinoids detected in the blood.

CAUSE OF DEATH

1a. Hanging

COMMENTS AND CONCLUSIONS

Taking all of the findings into consideration, it appears that this lady has died as a result of hanging. Although it was initially unclear at the time of the postmortem where the deceased had suspended herself from, review of scene photographs with which I was provided and following discussion with SAPOL Crime Scene, who attended the scene, it appears that the deceased has attached the spring clip of the dog lead to part of a metal beam on the garage roof, which has at some point become detached, with the deceased falling into the position in which she was located. Given that the ligature did not appear to be self-sustaining, this appears to have occurred close to or after death.

* * *

When Courtney read the report, it was the first time she had seen the authorities' conclusions about her daughter's death laid bare.

But it didn't hold all the answers about what happened to Rose. It couldn't. An autopsy is only supposed to reveal the medical cause of death.

The report did reveal that Courtney's initial concern – that police seemed to have deemed Rose's death a suicide before determining where she was hanging from – might have been correct. That was no consolation, though, when what she wanted was answers to her questions.

* * *

When Kathryn and Emily read the autopsy report, a couple of years after Courtney had received it, they had questions too. It was the first time they had heard any reference to Rose threatening self-harm.

They asked Courtney if she had known Rose to have mental health issues.

'You'd never got the impression from her that she was at risk?' Kathryn asked.

Courtney shook her head.

'I believe she would have rung triple zero if she was that level of suicidal. She would have known that she needed to be hospitalised, you know, and get some professional help,' she replied.

'The year before she died, her best friend had hung herself in a shed.

'Rose was out there after that with her friend's mum, raising awareness for suicide prevention. She always swore black and blue that she would never ever do anything like that herself.'

The team would later learn that Rose did have a history of mental health concerns. A few years before she died, she had been admitted to hospital after calling her mother and threatening to 'throw herself off a bridge'. But Courtney said her daughter did not 'mean it in that way'.

'We had a big fight once and she stormed off. She's like, "I'm gonna go and throw myself off a bridge."

'But that's her expressing herself, that's how expressive she is. To me, if she was going to go and do something like that, actually commit suicide, she would tell us.'

At the time of her death, there was a small amount of cannabis and an antidepressant in Rose's blood. When she died, she weighed just forty-five kilograms.

DYING ROSE

* * *

Courtney had never stopped asking questions of the police. Since December 2019, she had gone to the police station multiple times to raise concerns about the investigation or present evidence she had gathered.

Each time, Courtney said, she was told by officers to put her concerns into an email.

One of her greatest frustrations was that they had taken items belonging to Rose – among them her phone – but hadn't returned them, despite what she perceived as their complete lack of interest in pursuing her daughter's case any further.

On a cloudy grey morning, almost three years after Rose died, Courtney called Kathryn.

'Are you free today?' she asked. 'I'd like you to come to the police station with me. They're going to give me Rose's phone.'

As they drove to the station, Courtney told Kathryn what they'd be retrieving: a pair of earrings she'd given Rose on her sixteenth birthday, her daughter's ID, a letter or parcel, a laptop Rose had recently bought and, of course, her mobile phone.

Courtney said she was looking forward to seeing the photos on the phone. 'Rose loves to take photos,' she said. 'So there'll be a lot on there, you know?'

Kathryn felt apprehensive. Despite telling Courtney they did not believe there were suspicious circumstances surrounding Rose's death, it had taken the police three years to release her belongings. Kathryn wondered why it had taken so long, and what Courtney might be about to find out.

'We've been asking for these things for ages – it makes you feel like you're just not a priority,' Courtney told her. 'We wanted to go through that mobile phone right from the beginning. Even if it is a suicide, the trauma that's created for victims by not being able to view evidence … It's ridiculous. Three years for us not to be able to view any of that stuff.'

When they arrived, police handed over Rose's personal effects in a plastic bag.

By the time they left the station, heavy rain was beating down, and they hurried back to the car. It drummed on the windscreen as Courtney plugged Rose's phone into the charger.

Kathryn watched as Courtney began to rummage through the plastic bag. Among Rose's belongings was a note, written in neat handwriting. It read:

Why am I like this? They're using/manipulating me.
What's wrong with me? What have I done to deserve
this? Would people care if I was dead?

Kathryn glanced at Courtney, trying to gauge her reaction.

'There were post-it notes like this stuck all around Rose's room,' Courtney said, her exasperation audible. The others had little positive affirmations on them, she said. 'But they've only taken *this* fucking one.'

Courtney turned to Rose's phone, which had just blinked back to life. There was a small amount of dried blood at the bottom corner of the screen.

She began going through the phone's contents and soon found a series of text messages between Rose and Jared that had started just before 8 am on the morning of Rose's death.

In total, they had exchanged more than five hundred messages that day.

Courtney started reading the messages for the first time. She read them out loud, sometimes responding to them with comments of her own. 'That's bullshit!' she said a few times, shocked and disbelieving. Kathryn was also shocked by the messages: she got the sense Rose had been worn down and that she'd had enough of the volatile relationship.

It was clear she and Jared had fought that morning, just as Amy had recalled.

At 7.55 am – when the messages began – Rose told Jared: *You're fucked up. You're a little boy that can't even fucking say sorry.* She said she was going to go through his things and smoke all his weed.

Jared replied, telling Rose that her texts were 'evidence', and that if he arrived home to find his belongings missing, he would use the texts to report her to police.

Rose said she didn't care.

You chose this. You fucked me over and this morning was walking proof. You want to smoke all my shit but you wanna hide ur shit when it comes to you?

As the exchange continued, Rose's rage appeared to escalate as Jared responded less and less frequently.

During the exchange, Rose also called Jared forty-five times.

Finally, after hundreds of messages back and forth, Rose said she was leaving and that she was taking Phoenix with her.

No one has ever hurt me the way you have. I wish I never met you. You wanna treat me like this? Say ciao to the both of us. You have taken every single thing I have. So I'm taking it all back.

Jared replied: *Whatever. Wow. That's immature. Typical female.*

Rose responded: *No, it's not. I just don't wanna walk away with fucking nothing. You've literally drained everything out of me.*

Jared threatened to report her to police if Phoenix wasn't there when he got home.

Rose replied: *You deserve nothing.*

LOL ok, he responded. *Have fun you pretty thing.*

Oh if you find me dead, that's an extra bonus for ya too, Rose told him. *Just a heads up. Maybe I should kill myself?*

You're fucked, Jared replied.

Rose tried to call him then, but he didn't pick up.

That's how much you care, she wrote. *There is blood everywhere. You never cared. You don't care. You never did, never have.*

I swear to god I will call an ambulance, Jared replied.

Courtney stopped scrolling and took a breath, trying to steady herself. 'Why didn't he call a fucking ambulance?' she said, her voice shaky.

Rose told Jared he'd had his chance to listen and he was *fucked up, bad*.

Jared said he had started work. *Leave me alone*, he wrote.

Over the next four hours, Rose sent him more than a hundred more messages. Among them were photos. First, a photo of her wrist in the bathroom. Then, a photo of scissors.

One cut, two cuts, three. If I'm dead by the time you finish work, it's your fault.

No reply.

Maybe I should just die then. Then everyone would love me, hey? I'm gonna do it.

No reply.

Her three last messages to him came in quick succession.

Who cares about Rose, right? Let's just use her, right? Let's just use the fuck out of her and not hear what she has to say when she's angry? Right?

Let's let Rose kill herself, right? Let's let Rose feel this way? Right? Well I'm close.

At 3.38 pm, Jared sent his next message.

If my money or Phoenix isn't there, I will be reporting you to the police. I'm on my break, coming back now. You better have not taken anything.

Since you have stolen my money, I will be taking your earphones til you pay me the $95 you owe me. Oh also have fun getting your stuff.

When he didn't get an answer, Jared sent another message. *Where are you Rose?*

* * *

The texts on Rose's phone were fairly conclusive evidence that Jared had, in fact, been at work when she died. If it had been returned to the family earlier, it might have assuaged at least some of their concerns about what had happened to Rose. But none of the agencies the family dealt with seemed to think that their concerns mattered – or at least that's how it felt to Courtney, and to Mandy too. The authorities gave them the impression, whether it was accurate or not, that they had conducted their investigations only in order to fulfil their professional duties, and not for the benefit of Rose's family. Having satisfied themselves that there had been no foul play, that was enough: they felt no need to satisfy Rose's family on that point.

In the course of their investigation, Kathryn and Emily contacted SA Police, asking why they had not searched for CCTV recordings of Jared on the way to work on the day that Rose died, to confirm his whereabouts. They also asked if any further investigation into Rose's death had been undertaken after her family raised concerns, and why, if Rose's death was immediately ruled a suicide, Courtney had only been able to retrieve her belongings three years later.

Police declined to provide answers to any of these questions.

Kathryn and Emily then asked for a sit-down interview with a member of SA Police to discuss the case. This request was also declined.

A spokesperson for SA Police responded with a statement instead:

> SAPOL takes very seriously the investigation of any sudden death. These matters were investigated, which found no suspicious circumstances. The matters are now with the coroner and any further questions should be directed to the coroner's office.

When the reporters wrote to the South Australian coroner, asking about Rose's death and for any files relating to it, the coroner's office declined their request, saying it could not provide any details as the case had not gone to inquest.

* * *

In July 2023, Kathryn went to Campbelltown to pick up some documents from Courtney.

While at the house, she discovered that Courtney still had the phone she had found stuffed into a hole in Jared's bedroom wall – the one with the name 'Dying Rose' in the contacts list. It was an old, white Android – the type you could buy in a service station for no more than a hundred dollars. There was a crust of brown gunk on the bottom-left corner, and the screen was cracked through the centre.

Kathryn asked Courtney if she could try charging it – this time with a different charger.

The battery gasped into life, but the phone wouldn't turn on straightaway. Kathryn decided to leave it on charge. She wanted the best possible chance of seeing what was on it.

Two days later, Kathryn returned to Courtney's house, bringing Emily with her.

Courtney had told both reporters – time and time again – about the violent words she believed Jared had written using the phone's notes app before Rose's death.

Having been shocked by Rose and Jared's final text messages to each other, they weren't sure what they would find on that phone.

They checked the notes app first. It was packed with what appeared to be rap lyrics, full of violent imagery and phrasing and references to drug use.

Then they searched the contacts list.

Courtney had, for the past eighteen months, told them that Jared had listed her daughter under the name 'Dying Rose'.

When they opened the contacts app, Dying Rose was there, but the phone number associated with the name didn't belong to Courtney's daughter.

DYING ROSE

Jared had last texted the number nine months before Rose died. He and Rose had met around six months before she died.

Courtney was puzzled. She speculated that Dying Rose might have been an ex-girlfriend of Jared's.

The reporters read through the messages Jared had exchanged with this unknown person. None of them seemed to relate to Rose Hunter-Hebberman in any way.

Kathryn and Emily tried calling the number, but it had been disconnected.

Over the course of the investigation, they also made multiple attempts to contact Jared, including calling him and door-knocking his last known address. They left two written notes and a number of phone messages asking if he would share his account of what happened on the day Rose died, but Jared had never responded.

There is no suggestion that Jared was involved in Rose's death, or in any wrongdoing, but Kathryn and Emily still wish they had been able to speak to him. Despite their best efforts, the story of Rose's last day is far from complete. Jared might perhaps have helped them to fill some of the gaps, bringing Rose's family nearer to something like closure.

Because Courtney wasn't satisfied with the answers she'd received from the authorities yet – far from it.

'Our family is really strong,' she says. 'We're from the Hunters … my mother was a strong Hunter woman, and

I'm a strong Hunter woman too.' Rose was another strong Hunter woman, she said – and Courtney just didn't believe that her daughter would 'go knock herself', eradicating her own future.

'I tried to tell the cops at the beginning that I didn't believe she killed herself. I said, "No, there's no way that girl did … no way in hell,"' Courtney said.

'When the state tells me I'm wrong, that I don't know my child, that their system knows my child better than me – that undermines my whole identity.

'It undermines who you are as a black person,' she said.

* * *

If Rose Hunter-Hebberman had been crying out for help, no one listened. Her boyfriend didn't respond to her final messages, and no one knows for sure how she died.

Rose's mother, Courtney, may never find out what happened to her. All Courtney knows for certain is that the law didn't listen to her family when they most needed to be heard.

But although Rose would never know it, her story – and her mother's relentless fight to make it heard – would soon bring to light a national shame.

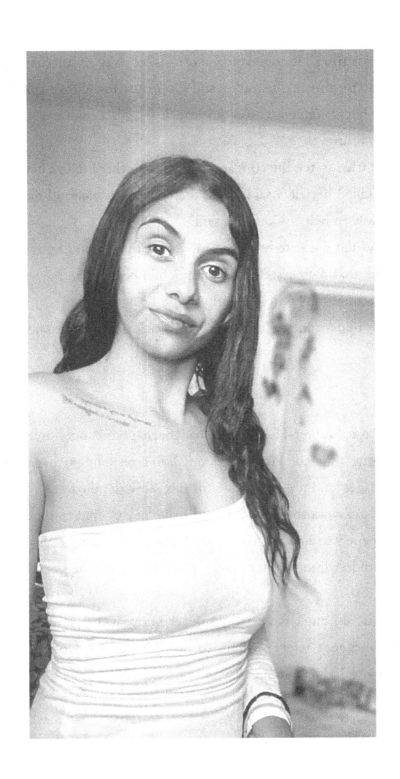

CHARLENE WARRIOR

On Saturday 18 September 2021, at about 8.30 pm, Charlene Warrior made a video call to her sister, Theresa. She was screaming and crying, pleading for help. All Theresa could see was Charlene's face, surrounded by darkness. She looked terrified.

Charlene had sent Theresa an urgent message on Facebook the day before, asking her family to come and pick her up.

Would yous do a night trip here, it read. *I need to run away with daughter.*

Now Charlene was hysterical, crying and crying. 'I just want to come home,' she sobbed.

She was on a park bench somewhere in the middle of Bute, a small farming town on the northern Yorke Peninsula in South Australia. There aren't many reasons to go to Bute – it's a quiet place, with one local store and a post office down the main street – but for Charlene, the drawcard was her one-year-old daughter, who lived there with her father, Charlene's ex. Charlene was visiting, staying at her ex's place.

Theresa was in Adelaide, nearly 150 kilometres away. She felt frightened and helpless. She was nineteen years old at the time, and Charlene was her best friend, the person she trusted the most. She told her sister to go back to her ex's place, pack her bag and wait for morning so she could leave with her baby daughter. They would try to find a way to get her and the baby home.

Charlene told Theresa that she was going to do exactly that.

Theresa wasn't sure what to think after her sister hung up.

Later that night, Charlene messaged Theresa again: *I hate this, literally the saddest shit ever.*

Theresa tried to call her, but she didn't pick up.

Theresa tried to call her sister again on Sunday morning and repeatedly throughout the day. 'I kept calling and calling her,' she said later, 'but she never got back.'

That was when, frantic with worry, Theresa had raised the alarm, getting friends and family involved, trying to track down her sister.

She even messaged Charlene's ex.

Theresa was too anxious to sleep and stayed up late, scrolling Facebook. In the early hours of Monday morning, she sent Charlene a song: it would remind her of Theresa, she said.

Charlene replied at 3.38 am, saying, *Probably reminded you of me.*

Theresa was relieved. *Nah,* she responded, less than a minute later, and then tried to call Charlene again, but she didn't pick up.

When she woke up later that morning, Theresa tried to call her sister again, but she still wasn't answering her phone.

Charlene's ex replied to Theresa's message later that day. He told her that he'd woken that morning to find Charlene gone and assumed she'd returned to Adelaide.

When Theresa told her family, some of them went to the rundown bus stop in the Adelaide CBD, hoping Charlene might step off the bus and her silence would prove to be a big misunderstanding.

'Hey, sis, you scared us,' Theresa might have said, as Charlene sheepishly explained her phone had just run out of charge on the trip home.

But Charlene wasn't on the bus.

'She'd just vanished,' Theresa said.

* * *

Every dark night has a brighter day.

Charlene Warrior had these words tattooed across her collarbone, an expression of her faith in the future, her certainty that something better was waiting for her, if she just fought on.

She'd had some difficult times: turbulent relationships, periods of homelessness and brushes with illicit drugs. At twenty-one, she had been trying for years to get her life on track, but Charlene had never surrendered. It seems fitting, in retrospect, that her last name, like her mother Alma's, was Warrior.

When Charlene's family described her, the first thing they said was that she loved being a mother. When she was with her baby daughter, she radiated joy.

She had fallen pregnant at nineteen to a man she barely knew, but even at that age, she knew being a mother was what she wanted. And not just any mother – Charlene wanted to be a really good mother.

She'd realised she was expecting towards the end of 2018, while she was in Melbourne over Christmas. Charlene didn't exactly tell her family back in Adelaide, instead leaving them to guess when she uploaded a picture of herself to Facebook, with a swelling belly and fuller breasts than usual.

'There's something wrong here, my daughter – you've been eating a lot. You're putting on a bit of weight,' her mother Alma told her.

When Theresa saw the photo, she thought, *Hey, her stomach looks a little bit big there.* She left a comment saying, 'You look pregnant.'

When Charlene deleted her comment, Theresa called her sister, gently nudging her to come clean. 'When I asked her,' Theresa said, 'she just broke it to us that she was really happy, over the moon. She came back home and told everyone she was pregnant.'

Her father, Kent Newchurch, had always called Charlene his 'little princess' and was delighted she was about to have a princess of her own. Alma and the rest of the family were overjoyed too.

Charlene had a tattoo on her lower left arm which read *Family is forever*. She had grown up in a tight-knit community, cared for not just by her mum and dad but by her aunties and uncles too. She'd been surrounded by people who loved her, with a deep connection to their shared culture. Alma and Kent both belonged to the Narungga people, whose traditional country is South Australia's Yorke Peninsula, across the St Vincent Gulf from Adelaide. The family had deep ties to 'the Station', the community at the former Aboriginal mission station at Point Pearce. Kent also had Kaurna ancestry, connecting him to the people of the Adelaide Plains.

That's what Charlene wanted for her daughter: to grow up surrounded by family and love, knowing who she was, secure in her culture and identity.

In the early days of her pregnancy, life was uncomplicated and Charlene was overrun with simple joy – but as the months went on, things became harder.

There is a photo of a pregnant Charlene with her sister Theresa standing by her side, taken by a professional photographer. Charlene wanted to show off her baby bump and let her family and friends know just how excited she was that she was going to be a mother. It's a beautiful image: the two sisters are standing together on a beach under the night sky, Theresa looking into Charlene's eyes as she smiles with pride. Charlene looks like it's one of the happiest moments of her life. What you don't see in the photo are the tears she wiped from her eyes just minutes before it was taken. Her baby's father was there that day, and he and Charlene were arguing because he didn't want to be in the photo with her. Luckily for Charlene, Theresa was there for her, like she'd always been, ever since they were small.

The family home was badly overcrowded, noisy and chaotic, and as her pregnancy progressed, Charlene couldn't cope with the stress. She moved into Malvern Place, a centre in the northern suburbs of Adelaide that caters to young pregnant women who would otherwise be homeless. The centre offers parenting education and help to find housing, though that could be difficult: Adelaide was in the middle of a housing crisis, with the lowest rental vacancy rate of any city in Australia at the time. Charlene also received support from a social worker at Ngangkita Ngartu, the Aboriginal Family Birthing Program at the Women's and Children's Hospital in North Adelaide.

Records show that Charlene had been trying hard to get her life in order so that she could be the best mum she could to her baby. But she had experienced a lifetime of challenges herself.

She had been witness to violence, exposed to others' drug and alcohol misuse and had experienced verbal abuse and threats of violence in her relationships. Her childhood was difficult at times, resulting in some early interactions with police. She had also been reported missing twice: the first time when she was just eleven years old and the second at age twelve.

Just over a year before her baby was born, Charlene had presented to a medical centre and spoken with a doctor who referred her on for specialist help. The doctor's notes make for sad reading. Charlene was stressed, homeless, looking for a job, unsure of what to do and very anxious. Around the same time, she had been prescribed an antidepressant. She left the medical centre with a provisional diagnosis of depression, but she had said clearly that she was not experiencing suicidal ideation at that time.

Not long after that, Charlene filled in another form, at the hospital where she'd give birth, this time affirming that she was not depressed; had no history of mental illness, and no history or thoughts of self-harm; had never suffered sexual or physical abuse, and had experienced no recent significant losses which could affect her mental health. The hospital was no doubt looking for signs she might suffer pre- or postnatal depression, as they would with any soon-to-be mother who came through their doors for antenatal care, but it is interesting that Charlene said she was not depressed when she had sought help so recently.

Whatever the true state of her mental health at that point, what shone through was Charlene's commitment to trying to improve her circumstances. But her life mirrored those of so many young First Nations people born into disadvantage, who often need remarkable resilience just to survive.

When Charlene's baby was born in August 2020 at the Adelaide's Women's and Children's Hospital, she was showered with affection by her proud new mother and the entire Warrior Newchurch clan. Despite what Charlene lacked in money and material things, she and her family were never short of love.

But Charlene wanted more than that for her baby. She desperately wanted financial stability: enough money to put a roof over their heads and buy food and pay bills without having to struggle. She knew the pain of poverty and disadvantage, and she didn't want that for her daughter.

She wanted to give her daughter the best life she could.

This desire both drove her and dragged her down. Charlene was her own harshest critic, and what she saw as her failures as a parent distressed her deeply. One of these failures in particular had distressed her beyond measure: she had struggled to find permanent housing for herself and her child.

In May 2021, when her baby was nine months old, Charlene sent her to live in Bute with her father, Charlene's ex, who lived there with his own father. She thought of the arrangement as temporary, a way to get a roof over her daughter's head while she tried to find a more satisfactory solution. Her plan was to get a place of her own and bring

Charlene Warrior

her daughter back to live with her as soon as she could. In the meantime, she would visit her once a month. She would have gone more often if she could, but Charlene was broke.

When her daughter first went to live in Bute, Charlene's ex came to pick them both up in a 'big white bus', which pulled up on the road in front of the Warrior Newchurch family's western suburbs home. The bus looked barely roadworthy, with the windows blacked out and the outside covered in a cheap coat of white paint. Alma Warrior says it was a 'strange-looking thing'. Inside were two men. Alma didn't know them, but they were her granddaughter's family. Charlene climbed aboard with the baby and they set off.

Bute is about an hour and forty minutes' drive north of Adelaide, at the top of the Yorke Peninsula, right on the boundary where the Narungga and Kaurna nations meet. Most people who visit tend to drive through without stopping. It's a small town, with a population of around four hundred, a place where everyone knows everyone, and locals either stick to themselves or meddle in others' business.

The quiet town felt foreign to Charlene, though she was born just half an hour down the road and had connections to the land from both sides of her family.

'We're from Yorkes, and we don't even know Bute,' as her sister Theresa put it.

Her ex's family home was humble: a typical outback South Australian property at the cheaper end of the market, with white fibro walls and modest fittings. The arid conditions meant there was no garden – just harsh dirt for a yard, complete with an old steel Hills Hoist clothesline and a pink plastic cubby house with a green roof, surrounded by a few pot plants. The lounge room opened straight onto the street, and the kitchen was basic, but it had three bedrooms, and the family kept it neat and tidy.

The monthly visits were uneventful. Charlene would take the bus from Adelaide to a town not far from Bute, where relatives would pick her up and drive her the final stretch. She would take her daughter for walks and to play in the park during the day and then sleep in her room with her at night, soaking up all the time she could with her cherished baby girl. Sometimes they'd go on family outings with her baby's dad.

It was, for a time, a workable arrangement, but Charlene couldn't bear to think of being separated from her daughter – her reason for being – over the long term. Her heart broke every time she had to say goodbye to her again before leaving to catch the bus home.

On 10 September 2021, Charlene had set off for Bute with one thought in mind – to bring her baby daughter back to Adelaide. She caught the bus, as usual, and then stayed the night with an aunt, who drove her into Bute the next day. Charlene liked to be dropped in town to walk the final stretch alone. Her family don't know why she didn't want them to drop her at the door.

At first it was like every other visit. Charlene did all the things she loved to do with her baby, and they went on outings together with her ex. At some point, though, things went wrong.

Charlene told her family she had been trying her best, but the baby had developed nappy rash. Charlene had been criticised for this, not by her ex but by someone he knew, and there had been an argument. She had been racially abused and called a 'black slut'.

It was on Saturday 18 September, a week after arriving in town, that Charlene had called Theresa from the park, alone in the dark and completely hysterical.

* * *

According to the family, Theresa reported Charlene missing to the police on or around Monday 20 September 2021. After several days went by and they hadn't heard anything, Charlene's parents, Kent Newchurch and Alma Warrior, went into the Port Adelaide police station in person to report their daughter missing on or around Friday 24 September. Theresa says she made another call on the following Wednesday, 29 September, at which point the police finally began working on plans for a search.

Theresa had ramped up her own search efforts the day before, using her phone to interrogate Charlene's ex. The two of them had traded messages on 28 September, and then again on 29 September.

Theresa told her sister's ex she had checked with the coachline, and Charlene hadn't been booked on a bus to Adelaide.

When she pushed him on Charlene's whereabouts, he told her: *I've got other shit on my mind such as your sister, so I ain't replying to your immature shit. If you have anything serious to say like if you hear from your sister or anything let me know, but besidez that don't contact me.*

He made it clear that his daughter would not be seeing her extended Warrior Newchurch family ever again – only her mother.

Theresa told him she was keeping screenshots of his texts and accused him of apathy. *You acting like you don't care that she is MISSING or probably dead*, she wrote.

Charlene's ex objected. *No that'z not alright*, he wrote. *Nothin iz on me, where ever she iz or what ever she'z done iz nothin to do with me.*

Theresa pleaded with him, asking where her sister could possibly have gone in such a small town with no money and no access to a car, and insisting that Charlene wouldn't leave her daughter behind.

Well that'z what she did, an have you seen the size of bute, it'z not even a town it iz small az, if she was round here I would ov seen her somewhere, he replied.

58

He said he had been at Kadina police station – police would later confirm he had been there on an unrelated matter – and he had learned that they intended to check Charlene's bank account to see if she had used her cards.

This was one of the first indications the family had that the police were treating Charlene's disappearance as suspicious.

* * *

On Friday 1 October, the police issued a press release and launched the official search for Charlene, using a Country Fire Service shed in Bute as their command post. SA Police officers, including members of the Mounted Operations Unit and the Special Tasks and Rescue Group, knocked on doors and scanned paddocks, vacant lots and buildings, coordinating their efforts with those of SES and CFS volunteers.

The next day, Saturday 2 October, Theresa fronted television cameras to tell Channel Seven news that she and her family needed all the help they could get from the public to find her sister, who seemed to have disappeared into thin air.

'There are fears a young Adelaide mum who went missing on the Yorke Peninsula has been murdered,' the newsreader said as she introduced Charlene's story.

A beautiful young woman, the mother of a sweet baby girl, had vanished in an outback Australian town and been missing for two weeks – yet that dramatic announcement was the first time the media had reported on her disappearance.

The news story was grave, showing vision of police and volunteers searching. It then cut to Theresa looking down at her phone, which showed a photo of her with Charlene in happier times, when her big sister was pregnant and glowing. The sisters' similarity was striking: Theresa looked so much like Charlene they could have been mistaken for twins.

'We haven't heard from her, her phone's been off, and we just need any information that we can get at this point,' Theresa told the TV cameras, barely holding her composure. Her voice shook, and she was visibly upset.

She explained that there was no way Charlene would just disappear, leaving her daughter behind. That was why the family feared for her safety.

'She loves her daughter more than life itself,' Theresa said. 'Her daughter is her world.'

The police pulled back their search that same evening, after just two days, having failed to find any sign of Charlene.

* * *

When Theresa appeared on the news, she and her parents believed Charlene had met with foul play and that police were treating her disappearance as suspicious. The police were in fact investigating the possibility Charlene had been the victim of a crime: although the family didn't know it, SA Police's Major Crime Investigation Branch, responsible for investigating homicides, had been consulted as the search for Charlene began.

But they didn't pursue that line of investigation for long.

On the evening of Sunday 3 October, police arrived at the family's home in the western suburbs of Adelaide to deliver shattering news.

Charlene Warrior was dead.

She had been found hanging in a tree. It looked to be a clear-cut case of suicide, the police said.

Charlene's family would never see her again, or even have the chance to farewell her remains with dignity. Her body was so badly decomposed she had to be identified by her teeth, using dental records.

She had been hanging in that tree for two weeks.

The tree was right in the middle of Bute, and she'd been hanging there in plain sight – yet no one had seen her.

* * *

At 6 pm on the day after the police search was pulled back, a man had been out walking his dog when he looked up and saw Charlene hanging in a tree at the edge of paddock, just off Park Terrace, near the centre of town. The tree was about a hundred metres from the house Charlene had been staying at, not far from the CFS shed the police had used as their search command post.

The man who found her dashed to the shed to get help from the volunteer firies. There happened to be two police there at the time, both from the Electronic Crime Branch, analysing CCTV footage.

Those in the fire shed rushed to the scene, and the tree and paddock were cordoned off. Those who had left town the day before rushed back, and Crime Scene police from nearby Kadina set to work gathering evidence. They photographed the dry paddock, its flat expanse interrupted only by the large tree, from every possible angle.

According to the investigating officer's report, there was no other sign another person had been at the death scene.

There were no marks around the tree that would indicate Charlene was dragged there, and the police were 'unable to locate any marks, scratches, or missing bark of significance on the tree that would indicate a struggle or suspicious circumstances relating to the deceased body being placed in the tree'.

The report also noted that, although she was small and slight, weighing only forty-one kilograms, it would have been impossible for another person to carry Charlene up the tree, conscious or unconscious, without leaving marks on her body. None were immediately obvious.

Based on all of that, the police ruled out lynching.

Charlene Warrior

Their theory was that Charlene had left her ex's house in the middle of the night, jumped a wire fence and walked across the paddock to the tree, where she hanged herself. The police concluded, on the basis of their interviews and research into Charlene's history, that she had been suffering from undiagnosed, untreated depression and that, in the days leading to her death, she had been distressed that her own homelessness, possible drug use and general circumstances meant she couldn't have her daughter live with her, so she took her own life. She had not been subjected to physical harm in Bute, the report said, but had likely suffered emotionally.

The investigating officer was of the view Charlene was responsible for her own death and that everything at the scene indicated suicide. The pathologist's postmortem autopsy report supported that view.

* * *

It was the *Advertiser*'s Indigenous affairs reporter, Douglas Smith, who first went to speak with Charlene's family after she disappeared, although back then he was working for National Indigenous Television, better known as NITV. Douglas had family connections to the Warrior Newchurch clan, and Charlene's father, Kent, especially.

'My dad and Charlene's dad grew up together,' Douglas explains. 'When Charlene went missing, my dad rang me up

DYING ROSE

and said the person who is missing, Charlene – her father is your uncle.'

For Douglas, Charlene's death was tragic news, but not shocking. Tragedy had stalked him throughout his life, in the way it stalks so many First Nations people.

He discovered he lived just a few streets from Kent and Alma and began to spend time with them at their home. Douglas met the whole family: Charlene's older brothers, Clifford and Kent Jr, her older sisters, Lena and Stella, and Theresa, the youngest.

Sitting in the lounge room, he listened to their stories about Charlene as a girl, growing up on Point Pearce at the Station. Theresa told him about going to the beach with their cousins and camping and fishing with their uncles and aunties, jogging memories of his own childhood. She talked about how they used to catch the bus to school and back together every day, and how Charlene loved playing netball. She was the best player in her team – a 'gun', just like her mum had been, Theresa said.

It was obvious how close she'd been to her older sister. There was just a year's difference between them, Theresa told him, and they'd been inseparable from the moment she was born. She said they knew almost everything about each other.

'I've never known life without her. It's a lot different now to live our lives, because she was the closest one to me out

64

of all my siblings,' Theresa said. 'It's a lot harder to do life without her.'

The way Alma has decorated their lounge room makes it obvious that the family have always been a tight unit: photos and memorabilia cover the walls and there are shelves of family photos too. One shelf is full of photos of Charlene. When you look at them, you see how much Alma loved her – and how much Charlene loved her own daughter, who is with her in many of the images. Being a mother suited Charlene, her family say, and the photos show the woman she became as she grew into her new role: she was loving and caring, and all about her baby daughter.

When Charlene disappeared, Theresa released two of these photos to the media. The first was the professional portrait of the two of them on the beach together, when Charlene was pregnant: the happy expectant mum and excited soon-to-be aunt. Charlene is wearing large gold hoop earrings and a tight white dress, her long hair straightened, looking glamorous. Theresa, who wasn't expecting to be in the photo, is in torn jeans and a cropped black t-shirt, her curls bobbing around her shoulders. They are both cradling Charlene's growing baby bump.

The second photo Theresa chose shows Charlene holding her daughter in her arms, her cheek nestled against her baby's happy face. They look besotted with each other and as happy as any mother and baby could be together. The simple beauty and happiness draw you in – and make the tragedy of their imminent permanent separation all the sadder.

There is something striking about both of these photographs, which would come to symbolise Charlene's life and the tragedy of her death in the minds of South Australians. Those images introduced us to Charlene as her family saw her: a beautiful, doting young mother.

Douglas remembers Alma sitting on the couch next to him, a photo of Charlene in her hand and tears in her eyes. 'All she cared about was her daughter,' Alma told him. She said Charlene's child had been the only constant in her life.

It didn't make sense to Alma, or any of the family, that she would have chosen to end her life, leaving her baby behind.

They feared Charlene's death had been written off too quickly – *Here's another black girl that's taken her life* – and they were still agonising over painful questions that had been left unanswered.

After joining the *Dying Rose* team, Douglas invited Charlene's family to visit the audio studio of the *Advertiser* to recount her story. Charlene's would be the first of the six stories we produced about the sudden deaths of young First Nations women. We hoped to help her family find answers to at least some of their questions, and to reach an audience who would, finally, make them feel that someone was listening.

* * *

Charlene Warrior

More than a year after the awful day they learned Charlene had died, Alma Warrior, Kent Newchurch and their daughter Theresa sat down with Douglas in the studio, thick black microphones in front of them, and told him about the events leading up to Charlene's disappearance.

In the days before she died, Charlene had come to the distressing conclusion she would have to leave her baby in Bute and head back to Adelaide without her. The problem was she didn't even have the twenty dollars she needed for her bus fare to Adelaide. Getting herself out of town and back to her family – let alone spiriting her daughter away with her – had begun to feel like a distant prospect. Theresa said Charlene had asked her for the money, but she didn't have twenty dollars.

What happened next has been pieced together from the accounts of people who saw Charlene, or spoke to her, and from phone records.

When Theresa wasn't able to lend her the money for her bus fare, Charlene sent a plea via Facebook Messenger to another relative, asking if she could lend her the money or come and pick her up by car. By midday on Saturday, they were on a video call together. The relative said Charlene 'looked very anxious'. She had her baby on her lap, and her eyes were red and puffy, like she had been crying.

The relative agreed to lend her the money – not realising it was already too late to help Charlene that day, or even the next day, as there were no buses from Bute to Adelaide on weekends.

By around 4.30 pm, Charlene was already in the park: police found two photographs on her phone of her daughter wanly sitting on playground equipment, taken moments apart, at 4.37 pm. Charlene must have taken her daughter home to her ex's house at some point after that, because when she spoke to Theresa in the park later that evening, she was alone.

Charlene called an aunty just before 7 pm and told her she was homeless in Bute and had taken refuge at the park. The aunty and her husband started trying to find someone to go to Charlene's aid. The relative who had earlier agreed to lend her the money realised then that there were no buses to get Charlene back to the city until Monday morning and tried to arrange for her to be picked up by another family member.

It was getting late, and Charlene was still in the park, alone, with no help at hand.

As a young Indigenous woman, she may well have been reluctant to call police for help, no matter how frightened and desperate she felt, fearing how the situation might play out. But even if she had called the police, the nearest stations were in Kadina, about a twenty-minute drive west of Bute, which is only open during business hours, and Snowtown, where opening hours vary, about twenty minutes to the east. If Charlene had called, and if a patrol car had happened to be nearby and was free to respond, perhaps the events of that weekend might have played out differently, but there is no way to know. It might have saved her life, or it might not.

A local in Bute called a Country Fire Service volunteer at 7 pm, asking if the volunteer could rush into town because, according to the police report, 'There was a girl that had an argument with her boyfriend and had been dropped off at one of the parks in Bute. He was told her name was Charlene.' She had told this man, or possibly another local, that she was unable to return to the house she had been staying in. She also told them she didn't know another soul in Bute.

The volunteer firefighter grabbed his partner and dashed into town, where they checked the public toilets, parks and playgrounds for Charlene. The local who had called him was also driving around the town looking for her, by now with a female companion, and two other men had also been roped in to try to find this mystery girl Charlene.

But the search party, though thorough, never found Charlene, and eventually a tip was called through, saying that she had returned to the home where her baby lived, and that she was safe.

Police records show that at 7.30 pm that night, Charlene was still in the park. By this stage, she was hysterical.

She then made another call, this time to a member of her ex's family, who told police later that she sounded 'distressed, upset and confused'.

At 8.30, Charlene made the call to Theresa that will haunt her for the rest of her life.

Charlene wasn't just crying; she was screaming and begging. 'That's all I want to get out of my head,' Theresa said, 'her scream, because she was screaming. She was just screaming and crying, saying, "I just want to come home."' Though they exchanged a few messages after that, it would be the last time the sisters ever spoke. Theresa never heard Charlene's voice again.

She still has flashbacks to that phone call.

After her distressed call to her sister, Charlene later called yet another relative, saying that she was homeless in Bute and was still in the park. This relative also started scrambling to get someone with a car to the town to collect her.

It's not clear what happened after that.

Her family say they are left wondering what happened to her in the hours and days following, because from that point on, there are fewer fragments to work with.

* * *

On Sunday 19 September, Charlene didn't answer any of Theresa's calls, making her sister frantic.

There was one sighting of her that day, just before midday, by a volunteer collecting information for the census who knocked on the door at her ex's place. He told police the

Charlene Warrior

woman he saw had a collarbone tattoo and was holding a baby. Charlene had a collarbone tattoo, and the census collector told police he believed it was her he had seen.

'Everything appeared okay' inside the house, he apparently reported.

By the early hours of the following morning, Charlene would be dead.

* * *

It was approaching midnight when screams pierced the quiet of the night in Everard Street.

A woman was wailing and shrieking in the street, and a male voice could be heard trying to reason with her.

There are only twelve streets in Bute. The town is so small that any unusual noises at night attract attention.

'I heard her screaming incoherently,' an older woman across the street would later tell the media. 'Screaming at the top of her voice, sobbing. Someone was with her, trying to calm her down, but she was screaming.'

Charlene was still missing when the woman talked to the TV reporters. Her body hadn't yet been found.

The woman lived directly opposite where Charlene had been staying. She had met the young mother when she had come to stay previously, but she did not know her well.

71

On the night Charlene vanished, the neighbour had gone to bed and heard people outside her window. A woman had been sobbing: 'an inconsolable type of cry'.

Worried, the neighbour opened her door to check on the woman – but suddenly silence returned to quiet Bute. She shut her door.

The howling came at the precise time Charlene's ex later told police she had raised the prospect of taking their baby back to Adelaide with her. They'd been sitting in the lounge room, debating where the little girl should live. 'It wasn't an argument but more of a disagreement,' he said. He told officers Charlene was 'upset', but that she had agreed that their daughter should stay in Bute.

When police quizzed him on what the neighbour had said to the media about a woman shrieking on the street, he told them Charlene had been out the front screaming and yelling at one point that night. He claimed not to know why, or what time it had been, and said he'd told her to relax.

The ex said she'd been on the lounge using her mobile phone when he went to bed.

He had assumed that she later went to bed in their daughter's room, which had been her nightly ritual since she arrived.

He was the last person to see Charlene alive.

When he awoke at 8 am and couldn't find her, he immediately suspected she had left with their daughter. Instead, he found the bub in her cot.

He told police later he had tried to call Charlene – and in doing so discovered her phone was wedged in the lounge.

That should have rung alarm bells, her family say now. Who in this age goes anywhere without their mobile phone?

She'd left her meagre belongings behind too, in their daughter's room: her bag, an iPhone charger, headphones and a pair of thongs.

Theresa is still angry that Charlene's ex didn't report her missing then.

'You're the last person to see her. But you never reported her missing. The mother of your child. She goes missing from your house. You didn't contact us. You waited for me to contact you and asked where my sister was.'

He said he thought Charlene had left to go home to Adelaide.

* * *

It was around then that Theresa says she first reported Charlene missing herself.

Her past experiences with police made her fear they wouldn't take her concerns seriously, and she told them so.

'I felt like she wasn't important enough to the police for them to find her,' she said. 'I said that to them at the start, I said, "Listen, you need to find her, cause I know what it's like for Aboriginal young girls like us in the Yorke Peninsula. I know how much we mean."'

Theresa is adamant she made her report on or around Monday 20 September 2021, but police say there is no record of it.

When the family heard nothing back from them for a number of days, Kent and Alma then went into the Port Adelaide police station, where they again reported Charlene missing, this time in person.

The police also contest this. In fact, they say there is no record of the family contacting them until the following Wednesday, 29 September, which was when Theresa, feeling sick with anxiety and increasingly frustrated by their lack of response, says she called them again.

Police say they lost nine days in the search for Charlene because her family and her ex did not report her missing when she first disappeared. They say delays can cause them to lose evidence, including CCTV footage, and make it more difficult to find and interview witnesses. They also say that the 'tyranny of time' affects the accuracy of witnesses' memories.

The family rejects the police assertion that no report was made in the first nine days that Charlene was missing. They say it makes no sense, and it is easy to see why they feel this way. Though Charlene's ex was the last person to see her alive, Theresa was the last person to communicate with her, when they exchanged messages on Facebook in the small hours of the morning. Her last attempt to call her sister before she went to bed was at 3.41 am. If Theresa was concerned enough to be up in the middle of the night checking on Charlene, it seems unlikely she would then wait more than a week before reporting her missing to the police, at a time when she was putting so much energy into her own desperate search effort.

Charlene's ex also objects to the police attributing difficulties they faced in their investigation into Charlene's disappearance to any lack of action on his part. As he told detectives, he initially thought Charlene had returned home to Adelaide and was unaware she was missing until Theresa contacted him looking for her. At that point, having being in contact with Theresa, he presumably thought, as the family did, that the official investigation was already under way.

When the hunt for Charlene finally began, police searched his house. It was neat inside, and fresh laundry, baby clothes and toys painted a picture of his daughter's life there. It is not suggested Charlene's ex or anyone in his family had any involvement in Charlene's disappearance and death.

* * *

For the entire fifteen days her sister was missing, Theresa felt an emptiness inside. She had felt it ever since she'd last spoken to Charlene. It was like a piece of her was gone, almost as if her twin had left this world. She knew something was wrong – she could feel it.

She wasn't the only one in the family who felt that way. Alma told Douglas she'd had a 'funny feeling' of dread descend immediately when she was told her daughter was missing. 'I thought something must have happened to her, for her not to come back with her baby,' she said.

But none of them had been expecting it to be suicide.

When the police had descended on their home that day with the news of her sister's death, Theresa was furious.

'These police officers, they came with grieving pamphlets, and they told us my sister was in the tree, hanging,' she said. 'They told us how tall the tree was, they told us a lot of stuff about how she was found.'

How had they made their minds up so quickly? And how could they shut down their investigation when there was so much they still didn't know?

She took the pamphlets they offered her and tore them up.

'I ripped them up, I threw them on the ground, and I said get out of my yard.'

She said the discovery of her sister's remains had changed the investigation in an instant.

'After her body was found, the police were so distant. There wasn't that much communication and stuff, and it just went really quiet,' she said.

They family were in a state of shock. They felt more questions should be asked about the hours leading to Charlene's death and about the search for her.

Charlene Warrior

The day after Charlene's body was found, Theresa called the police to ask what they could share with her. She was searching for answers, as any family member would. It was still early days, and she didn't expect to get much straightaway. From her past experiences dealing with the authorities, she wasn't even sure if the police would speak to her.

'They transferred me to the grieving officer up in Port Augusta. He's an Aboriginal officer and he speaks to the grieving families,' Theresa said.

Port Augusta, a few hours north of Adelaide, is well known for the often difficult relationship between the police and local Aboriginal families.

'Listen,' she said to the officer. 'I know I'm young, but I'm not stupid. I know something is wrong here. I know what the cops are saying, that I'm a grieving person now because my sister's body has been found, but you personally, as an officer, what do you think of this?'

Theresa doubted he'd even listen to her, and the last thing she expected was that he'd actually acknowledge her concerns. Up until then, she felt as if no police officer had taken her seriously.

But his automatic response was, 'I'm going to tell you, Nunga to Nunga, if the case was classed as a suicide, Major Crime would not be involved. Just keep that in mind.'

What he was saying to Theresa was, 'I'm going to be straight with you, as one Aboriginal person to another: if the big guns are involved, we haven't ruled out foul play.'

Being Aboriginal himself, he could understand where she was coming from, and he also understood the barriers Aboriginal people have always faced when they try to speak to police. But it wasn't just about lived experience and cultural understanding. It was about the feeling of cultural responsibility Aboriginal people have for each other. With a body found and Charlene's death confirmed, the officer knew he had to look out for Theresa and her family.

It was the first time in her dealings with the police that Theresa felt heard or believed. She knew she still had a fight ahead of her if she wanted answers. Yet there was another part of Theresa that expected she would be heard.

In her mind, there was clear evidence that the loss of her sister, her best friend, her most trusted person, was not the 'open-and-shut case' it had been treated as.

Now that she knew at least some of the police investigating the case agreed with her, she hoped her concerns, and those of her family, could be listened to and acted on.

* * *

Theresa wanted to know not just how her sister had died, but how she could have been missing in plain sight for so long.

Charlene Warrior

For a moment, let's approach the situation hypothetically. If you were investigating a missing persons case, and you found the missing person hanging in a tree, your first instinct would tell you that in all likelihood that person had died by suicide. It seems like the obvious conclusion.

But Charlene's body was found hanging extremely conspicuously in a tree on the edge of a paddock right in the middle of Bute, a very small town. She was likely visible, albeit somewhat obscured by trees and shrubbery, from the Country Fire Service shed the police had used as their search command post, and she could definitely be seen from the surrounding roads.

It's unbelievable that she wasn't found sooner. How did no one look up? Not police, not the volunteers in the search party and not the locals. No one looked up, not in the almost two weeks that police said Charlene had been in that tree. It is little wonder the minds of her family wandered to more sinister scenarios.

* * *

Months after Charlene died, SA Police agreed to a sit-down with the Warrior Newchurch family and a representative of the Aboriginal Legal Rights Movement.

The meeting took place at Tauondi College, an Aboriginal educational and cultural institute in Port Adelaide. Alma and Kent asked the police a series of questions about the investigation, hoping they would finally receive the answers they had been longing for. The police did answer some of their questions, in a written report that they provided after the meeting. For example, Charlene's mobile phone had a smashed screen, and the family wanted to know if that might indicate foul play. The police were able to rule out that line of enquiry: they had established that the screen had already been smashed for weeks before Charlene died.

But some of the 'answers' weren't answers at all.

The family had asked why there was no record of Theresa's first call to police, or of Kent and Alma's visit to Port Adelaide police station.

This was the police response:

SAPOL records indicate that Charlene Warrior was reported missing to police on the 29th of September 2021.

The family also wanted to know why the Warrior Newchurch clan wasn't spoken to. They were asking why the police hadn't kept them informed of the investigation's progress, or of developments in the case. In response, police provided a list of immediate and extended family members they had spoken to during the investigation, seventeen people all up – but they didn't address the actual question the family wanted answered.

Charlene Warrior

One of the biggest questions was this: why had police failed to see Charlene in the tree, when it was so close to their search command post?

The report said that from their vantage point at the CFS shed, Charlene's body had been obscured by shrubs.

The family weren't the only ones who found this unconvincing. In December, police returned to Bute to try to understand how Charlene could have been missing in plain sight for so long.

From some places tested by police, including the CFS shed, they said it would have been difficult or impossible to see Charlene hanging in the tree.

But after her body was found, officers had travelled east on the main drag, Martin Street. When they returned to Martin Street, they found that Charlene's final resting place would have been obscured in places by shrubs, but that there was a 'clear view' from other sections of the road.

* * *

Theresa went with Douglas, her father Kent and sister Lena back to Bute for the recording of the *Dying Rose* podcast episode dedicated to her sister. It was tough for her just seeing the picnic table in the local park where Charlene had been sitting in the dark that night, crying and screaming, the last time they ever spoke.

'She was sobbing,' an emotional Theresa recalled. 'This is where I told her, like, go back there, pack a bag.'

The table could have been in any park in Australia. Surrounding it were a playground, a public toilet block and a barbecue – all very ordinary.

They drove past Charlene's ex's house, the place she was last seen, and to a few other locations in town before they pulled up at the Country Fire Service shed. Kent, Theresa and Lena jumped out of the car to see for the first time where their beloved Charlene had died.

The shed the police used as their search command post is just a hundred metres from where her body was found. The family was shocked. No, more than shocked. They were completely horrified.

'There was no way she was in that tree and had no one see her. That's impossible,' Theresa said, her voice harsh.

'How could they miss someone in a white jumper?' Lena said angrily.

It was true: Charlene had been wearing grey tracksuit pants, white socks and a white jumper, and should have been highly visible.

It staggered her family that she could have been in that tree for thirteen days and no one in town had looked up, no searcher raised their eyes.

In theory, it was possible Charlene had been there the entire time from when the autopsy report said she died on 20 September to when she was found on 3 October. It had been an unusually cool spring in the usually baking, arid landscape of the Yorke Peninsula town of Bute. That may help to explain why a corpse out in the open drew no attention and nature didn't intervene to reveal the tragedy sooner.

But how could locals going about their business have missed seeing her for almost two weeks? And even more incredible: how could a dedicated police search of the area lasting two whole days have failed to discover her hanging there when the search headquarters was just a stone's throw from the paddock?

Seeing the site for themselves only raised more questions for the family.

Nothing about how SA Police said her sister died made any sense to Theresa, nor to the rest of the family.

But Theresa believed she had information that the police had not yet heard.

A local in Bute had confided in Theresa that she believed Charlene had not been in the tree for the entire two weeks.

A woman who worked in a local shop said one of her family members was part of a local volunteer organisation that helped with the search and claimed that Charlene's body was not in the tree while they had been conducting the search. She had apparently looked up into its branches but did not see Charlene in her distinctive white jumper.

Theresa had seized on this information and got in touch with the volunteer.

'Come down here, I'll speak to you,' the volunteer told her.

'Listen, what do you think about what happened to my sister?' Theresa asked her.

'All I know is that she wasn't there those days,' the volunteer said.

She knew the autopsy report said that Charlene had died around 20 September, and that the family had found out she was dead on 3 October.

'What I can say is that she was not there the day before that,' the volunteer said.

It is very possible that this volunteer was confused. Either way, what she told Theresa added to the confusion Charlene's family was already contending with.

* * *

During the course of the *Dying Rose* podcast investigation, the *Advertiser* acquired the police report into Charlene's disappearance and death compiled for the state coroner by the Port Pirie Police Criminal Investigation Branch. It reveals that on 30 September 2021, the local police had consulted SA Police's Major Crime Investigation Branch detectives.

Charlene Warrior

They had concerns about Charlene Warrior's disappearance and had briefed more senior police on the need for a 'full-scale search' for Charlene.

The officer who had contacted Major Crime wrote:

From the outset of my involvement in this matter and throughout the initial investigation, I considered Charlene Warrior's disappearance to be concerning and potentially suspicious.

The reasons for this concern included the fact that Charlene hadn't been seen since 20 September; that her phone and bank accounts were untouched; that she had not contacted family; that she had no money or car to leave Bute; and that she had left a child and belongings behind. The officer felt that the lack of a body 'added more weight to suspicions involving Charlene Warrior's disappearance'.

Major Crime took an interest in the case and were due to visit Bute on 4 October. In the meantime, police with other areas of expertise began investigating whether Charlene had taken her own life.

The report makes for sad and frustrating reading. Charlene didn't always rise above her struggles, and it contains more misery and horror packed into twenty-one short years than most people experience in a lifetime.

There was some evidence towards the end of her life that she had used drugs. Charlene's ex told police she had smoked pot and he thought she'd been 'getting on the ice a fair bit'. They also uncovered messages on her phone referring to 'gear' and 'pipes'. The messages were in both English and Kaurna, the language of the Adelaide Plains.

The views of Charlene's ex and the messages found on her phone do not prove beyond all doubt that she had become a drug user, and Charlene is not alive to contest that evidence, but it wouldn't be extraordinary if she had. The most recent figures available, for the period 2022–2023, indicate that more than one in four First Nations people had used illicit drugs in the previous twelve months and that they were more than twice as likely as non-Indigenous Australians to have used methamphetamine and amphetamine in the past year. The question, of course, is why Charlene might have turned to drug use.

Police also found videos on Charlene's phone and posts on her Facebook account in which she talked about depression. In one video, shot in August 2021, Charlene was sobbing, saying she was 'not good enough' for her little girl. Any objective analysis of all she had done to seek help since her daughter was born would say the opposite: this was a vulnerable young woman who had done her very best in difficult circumstances. It is clear, however, that she was struggling.

'Every night I cry to myself because I feel I'm failing my little girl … I never wanted life to be like this for us,' she said.

But the most deeply distressing discovery on Charlene's phone was a photo of her with her daughter, with the caption: *See you in the next life, know mummy always loved you my baby.*

The photo had been edited at 3.13 am on 20 September, the day the coroner ruled Charlene had died. This was a crucial piece of evidence supporting the investigators' conclusion that her death had been suicide.

* * *

The report also considered failings in the police response to Charlene's disappearance and the conduct of the official search.

A good search is planned well and launched quickly. It is thorough and relentless, and it generates wall-to-wall media coverage.

The search for Charlene was poorly planned, launched far too late, beset by problems and wound up far too quickly. Police conceded, in hindsight, that it should have been handled better.

While a better search would have done more to assuage the family's doubts, it would not have changed the outcome. Charlene would still be dead, no matter how well or otherwise SA Police conducted the search. But some of the reasons for their failure to find Charlene are shocking.

Some 'big dogs' lived at a property across the road from where Charlene was staying. Police openly state in their report that they declined to ask the owner – the neighbour who had heard Charlene sobbing on the night she died – to move them so that they could search her yard. She had warned them the dogs might react badly to males.

The dogs were confined in a poultry yard, which searchers were unable to enter and could only check visually, from outside, rather than searching. The yard was adjacent to the neighbouring paddock, and the chicken coop blocked the view of the tree Charlene was hanging in, which was right behind it. Police later described this oversight as 'unfortunate', when 'unacceptable' would be the more appropriate word. The excuse certainly didn't wash with the Warrior Newchurch family.

While they defended the search, police did concede that it would have been appropriate to request that the dogs' owner remove the dogs so that the chicken yard could be searched. In future, the report said, officers assigned to searches should be told at the outset to request any obstacles, such as dogs, be removed. Had police or volunteers entered the chicken yard, there is every chance they might have looked up and spotted Charlene.

The report also noted that the owner of the paddock where Charlene was found was in hospital dying. If he had been home, he would likely have spotted her: 'Unfortunately it is highly probable this gentleman may have discovered the deceased when checking his stock and paddock well before the date she was eventually discovered.' It later transpired the man had been dead for weeks. He had succumbed to a heart attack at Port Julia, more than an hour's drive from Bute.

An officer and five SES volunteers had been tasked with searching that area, but they had concentrated on the inner ring of their search zone and hadn't checked the man's paddock. In later searches, the guidelines were changed so that search zones overlapped, to prevent that situation arising again.

Locals close to the farmer's family were surprised that no one had seen Charlene's body in the thirteen days she had been hanging there. They said there had been 'more eyes on the paddock than ever' at the time, as relatives and friends had flocked to the farmer's home to console his widow and lend a hand tending to the property. It just didn't add up.

'When I saw what was written in the police report, about him being unwell, I thought, *That part isn't correct*,' a friend of the farmer's family said. 'They were insinuating that he wouldn't have been checking the paddock – but because he died suddenly, there was a band of people around there because it was such a heart-wrenching time.'

The reasons the police gave for failing to find Charlene – the dogs, the dying neighbour, the grid overlap issue – were flimsy. The force also sought to clear itself of the charge that its response to Charlene's disappearance or the subsequent search had been deficient.

While police ultimately blamed Charlene's transience for the delayed search effort, the report took aim at her family and friends, saying that although no criminal activity had been identified as contributing to Charlene Warrior's death, 'morally' there had been some missed opportunities to alert authorities to her disappearance earlier.

For a family already feeling let down by the police, this was a double blow.

The police were particularly strident in their response to the family's claim that Charlene was treated poorly because she was Aboriginal, rejecting this claim as 'completely unfounded and incorrect'. Instead, the report emphasised the racism Charlene had experienced from others, referring to the verbal abuse she had been subjected to not long before her death, when she had been called a 'black slut' by an associate of her ex's. It seemed likely, the report's author said, that she must have felt 'quite isolated, anxious and depressed at this time'.

Police rejected the 'misinformation, misguided advice and gossip' that were circulating, which they said were causing Charlene's family and the Indigenous community 'a significant amount of grief, anger and misunderstanding'. They also asserted that Charlene's family's unwillingness to accept that she had died by suicide had caused 'agitation', by which they meant that Black Lives Matter marches had been staged in Adelaide, protesting their treatment of Charlene's case and the apparent apathy of the wider South Australian community.

Many in the Indigenous community in Australia were following how Charlene's disappearance and death were handled – not only by the police, but by the media.

A few weeks before Charlene vanished, an American woman, Gabby Petito, was reported missing in the United States. The 22-year-old had been travelling across the US with her boyfriend, Brian Laundrie, when she vanished on 27 August 2021. She was later discovered dead in a national park in Wyoming. Laundrie had murdered her.

For the three weeks that Gabby Petito was missing, her story received wall-to-wall coverage in the Australian media and overshadowed Charlene's disappearance. It seems the media in Australia were more interested in the story of a missing 22-year-old white woman half a world away than a 21-year-old First Nations woman in her own country.

The difference in the way the media covered their stories angered many in the Indigenous community, and a Facebook post about 'missing white woman syndrome', contrasting the media's approach to Gabby and Charlene's disappearances, went viral. It said:

> What about missing 21-year-old Aboriginal woman,
> Charlene Warrior from Adelaide? She went missing only
> a week after Gabby … I mean the media didn't really
> cover much hey, in fact it wasn't until just a week ago
> that her story was put on mainstream media. Sadly, people

don't search tirelessly for people like me, people don't demand answers for people like me, our victimisation is normalised.

It was not just Charlene's family and members of the Aboriginal community seeking to draw attention to the deficiencies of the search. The Aboriginal Legal Rights Movement, an Indigenous legal service based in South Australia, appealed to the coroner to hold an inquest into the police response to Charlene's death, which the ALRM characterised as 'appalling' and 'disgraceful'.

But the coroner rejected the request.

'I think that the coroner was concerned that the cause of death was really not open to strong dispute,' an ALRM representative wrote, 'and that although the circumstances, particularly in relation to the search, were appalling, that was not sufficient to persuade the coroner that an inquest should be held.'

After years of turmoil, that was it. Case closed.

Yet the agony goes on for Charlene's family.

LASONYA DUTTON

It was about 10.30 am when Merle Dutton pulled into the front yard of his mother's house in his white Nissan Navara. It was oddly quiet. All the blinds were pulled down and the doors were shut. It looked like nobody was home but a few stray dogs. A strange feeling swept over Merle as he sat in the driver's seat, looking at the house so still and quiet.

Nanna Norm was a respected Elder in Wilcannia, a remote outback town in central-western New South Wales, and her place was usually abuzz with people coming and going all day. All were welcome at Nanna Norm's, whether they were relatives visiting from out of town or friends and family in the community who dropped in regularly for a cup of tea and a yarn. The door was always open.

The four-bedroom house sat on a small hill, surrounded by a spacious yard. Written-off cars and half-built motorbikes lined the front fence. Nanna Norm's sons, nephews and grandsons could usually be seen pulling cars and motorbikes apart in order to fix their own with spare parts. There was always something going on at the Dutton place.

The house was in the middle of what is known in Wilcannia as 'the Mallee', a part of the town where only Aboriginal families live. The main street that splits the middle of the Mallee is named Barkindji Drive, after the people whose country stretches from Wilcannia to the state border near the Riverland town of Renmark in South Australia.

Barkindji means 'people of the Barka' – the river known to most Australians as the Darling – and the Barkindji have relied on the flow of its water to sustain them through the generations. It is Australia's third-longest river, stretching a magnificent 1472 kilometres from northern New South Wales down through the middle of Barkindji country, connecting with the Murray River at Wentworth. The Barka had been dry for months, though – and as Merle's brother Keith said, when their river wasn't healthy, the Barkindji people suffered.

Merle had come to plan a hunting trip with Keith for the following night. He got out of the car and knocked at the front door to see if anyone was home. When he went to turn the handle, it was locked, so he went around the side of the house to try the back door.

There was a stray dog in the backyard, meddling with what Merle thought was a dead animal, in inch-high grass near the clothesline, maybe three metres from the house.

At first, he wasn't sure what he was looking at. 'I spotted a dog chewing on what I thought was a kangaroo,' Merle said, 'but it wasn't a kangaroo.'

He didn't think anything of it until he got up a bit closer, then the horror hit him like a freight train.

'I realised it was a human being,' he said.

He was looking at the dead body of his niece Lasonya, Keith's daughter. Her entire right foot and a large part of her lower right leg were gone, as if she'd been there for some time and several animals had been gnawing at her.

'I just ran out screaming and screaming,' Merle said.

Startled, the dog fled from the yard and ran off into the Mallee.

When Merle had managed to gather himself, he went back round into the yard and took a brief look at his niece's dead body.

He had never seen something so confronting. Her corpse had already decomposed almost beyond recognition.

Merle called triple zero to report his sickening discovery and then waited for the police.

Ten minutes later, the local police arrived.

Merle was expecting, as the person who had discovered Lasonya's body, that he would be questioned by police. What happened next still shocks him.

As they cordoned off the yard with tape, the police told Merle to leave.

He said they didn't ask him any questions, or request a statement from him.

'The only time I spoke to the police was when they told me to leave because it was a crime scene,' Merle said. 'I don't know what happened after that. If you ask me, it was like they were trying to sweep it under the rug.'

A woman had been found dead, mauled by dogs, in her family's own backyard – and the police just told Merle to go home. To this day, he can't understand why they didn't want to talk to him. He believed he had valuable information he could give them, but he was never asked about any of it.

* * *

On the day Merle found his niece's body, Tuesday 29 March 2022, her father, Keith Dutton, was two hours away in the outback mining town of Broken Hill. He had taken Nanna Norm there earlier that morning to receive dialysis for her diabetes, which she had to do three times a week.

He was at a friend's place when someone rang looking for him.

'They said something like: "Lasonya's been found dead in the back of your mother's place,"' Keith said.

They told him that she'd had an electrical cable wrapped around her neck, and about what Merle had seen.

Lasonya Dutton

'It was a bit hard to believe at first, and I didn't know how to tell Mum,' he said.

Keith was in shock. Lasonya was his only daughter. She was just thirty-one years old, still young, a happy-go-lucky mum of two, and she loved life. Family and friends called her a party girl. She had her troubles – it was no secret she had a problem with alcohol – but she was a loving daughter and a caring mother. People said she didn't have one bad bone in her body.

Keith didn't want to believe that she was dead, or to think about her body lying in the backyard, being eaten by dogs. He couldn't come to terms with how she had died, either. *Someone's done something to her*, Keith thought. Who would have wanted to hurt his daughter like that? He didn't return to Wilcannia until a couple of days later, unable to face the thought of it.

When he arrived home and saw exactly where Lasonya's body had been found, Keith was even more distressed and confused.

According to police, Lasonya had been dead for at least three or four days when Merle found her. That meant her body had been lying there just metres from the back door of Nanna Norm's house since the weekend.

It didn't make sense. How could she have been lying there so long without anyone noticing? It was a bustling family home, with people always coming and going. They'd all been in and out constantly over the past few days.

Keith found it especially baffling that his father hadn't seen Lasonya lying in the backyard in plain view of the kitchen window.

Trevor Jones – or 'Pop Footer' as everyone called him – was always home and only ventured out for his doctor's appointments.

Pop Footer never really talked much – he was more the deep-thinking type. If you walked inside the Dutton home, you could usually find him standing in the kitchen near the sink with a cup of tea in his hand, looking out into the backyard.

'My father spends twenty-three hours a day in the kitchen and dining area looking out of that window into the backyard,' Keith said. 'There's no way in the world he didn't see my daughter lying there for those three or four days or however long they said she was lying there.'

Pop Footer had left the house at 10 am on Tuesday, just half an hour before Merle discovered Lasonya's body, to go to the local hospital for a check-up – but on Saturday, Sunday and Monday, while Lasonya was apparently lying in the backyard, her body decomposing, he'd been home the entire time.

Lasonya couldn't have been lying there all weekend, Keith reasoned. But if her body wasn't there on the weekend, where had it been? And how had it appeared out of nowhere on Tuesday morning in his mother's backyard?

Lasonya Dutton

* * *

A group of NSW Police detectives were travelling up and down the Mallee, making inquiries. They were an unusual sight: according to Keith, the police and the town's Aboriginal community have never had a good relationship, and the local police tend not to go to the Mallee except when they're there to lock someone up.

Now there were police everywhere – but like the local police, the detectives weren't interested in taking a statement from Merle, and they weren't too keen to answer Keith's questions, either.

Wilcannia is a small town, with a population of about seven hundred. About half of that population is Indigenous – which meant that the Duttons were connected to nearly all of them, one way or another. Keith wanted to know who the police were talking to and what they were asking them, but the police kept fobbing him off.

Keith grew increasingly frustrated by the lack of communication. He wanted answers about what had happened to his daughter.

He began conducting his own investigation – asking those in the tiny, tight-knit town about his daughter's final days. Keith learned that there had been multiple sightings of Lasonya that weekend by people in the town. The accounts of the sightings were vague at best, and some were contradictory.

Few were certain exactly where they'd seen her, or whether she was with someone, or what time it had been. Keith also heard rumours of Lasonya being assaulted on the Friday night, a bloody knife found at the town's oval, and a bloody sheet at the tip.

Two of the last people to see Lasonya alive were her first cousins, Raelene and Katrina Hunter. Raelene and Katrina aren't sisters, but cousins themselves. The three women were very close, like sisters. Having known each other since they were very young, they shared secrets and stories with each other.

On the Friday before Lasonya's body was found, they had spent most of the day at Raelene and Katrina's grandmother's house on Barkindji Drive, a few doors down from Nanna Norm's, the three of them merrily downing drinks, sharing riotous laughter and enjoying each other's company. They were listening to country music – their favourite. Other family and friends also came and went, but the three women had been there together all day. Raelene and Katrina vividly remember Lasonya raving excitedly about an upcoming trip to Adelaide with her son, Baby Keith.

Baby Keith had lost his left foot in a motorbike accident the year before, and he had to go to the city regularly for doctors' appointments. Lasonya always went with him.

'I think it was the next week that she was leaving,' Katrina said. 'That's all she was talking about, was the trip that she had to do to Adelaide with her son for his foot.'

To Raelene and Katrina, it seemed like a good opportunity for Lasonya to get out of Wilcannia with just her son for a few days. Even though it was for a medical appointment, they all saw it as something to look forward to.

Lasonya sometimes struggled with caring for her children. Her friends and family knew this, but they also knew she was trying her best, and they tried to support her. In Aboriginal families, everyone pitches in to look after the kids: if he wasn't with Lasonya, Baby Keith was looked after by his grandfather or Nanna Norm.

As the day wore on and the sun started to set, Lasonya finished her last drink at about 6.30 pm, according to Raelene and Katrina, and decided it was time to head back to Nanna Norm's house, where she was living at the time.

'She said she was going home, and she was in a happy mood, like she didn't seem stressed about anything, because we enjoyed ourselves that day,' Katrina said. 'We were just having a good old time, us and a couple of other family members. We were all together. It came to the Friday afternoon, getting towards the evening, and she said, "Oh, my brothers and sisters, I'm going home now and I'll see you all tomorrow."'

She was heading just a few hundred metres down the road, but whether she got home or not is unknown.

* * *

What Keith most wanted to know was who his daughter had been with on the weekend before she was found dead – and if the rumoured sightings were true, she had been seen with a man on at least one occasion in the lead-up to her death.

After Lasonya left their grandmother's house on Friday night, someone told Raelene and Katrina, she had turned up at another house on Barkindji Drive in the Mallee. She was with a man, they said – someone she already knew. Keith said he knew the man too but hadn't ever spoken to him at length and, if he was being honest, didn't like him all that much. Both Lasonya and the man had apparently arrived intoxicated and were looking for a place to sit and drink.

It's not known just how long they were at the house on Barkindji Drive, but a man named Alan, a relative of the Dutton family, said he'd seen Lasonya in the town, about two kilometres away, walking down the main street late on Friday night. Alan said he'd been drinking and was sitting in front of the town hall, when he saw her.

'I was sitting on my own there, and 'ere sister girl coming, 'ere my two brothers, you know,' Alan said.

She was with the same man she had already been seen with that night and his brother. The three of them looked like they had also been drinking.

Alan said he didn't know what the time was then, but it was late.

104

Lasonya Dutton

Lasonya and Alan knew each other well and would usually stop and talk for a while before parting ways, but this had been a brief encounter. She asked for a smoke, he said, but he didn't have any. 'If I had a smoke, I would've gave you a smoke,' he told her.

She told him she was going home with the two men, and they just kept on walking straight up the road, he said. Alan thought she seemed a bit too drunk to be bothered talking.

'That was the last time that I seen her,' he said.

After hearing that Alan had bumped into Lasonya on the night she was last seen, Keith said he told the police about it. He voiced his suspicions about the man Alan had seen her with and wanted to know if the police were looking at him as a suspect.

He says he was told by officers 'not to worry and that they had it all under control'.

A year after Lasonya's death, Keith asked Alan if police had ever questioned him about his sighting of her, or asked about the man she'd been with.

'They never talked to me about that there brother. They never talked about it to me,' Alan said. 'They never asked me no questions or nothing. I was the last fella that seen her, fair dinkum ... I was the last fella that saw her.'

But while Alan believed he was the last person in the community to have seen Lasonya alive, there was apparently one more sighting of her.

At about 2 am on Saturday, one of Keith's relatives was driving into town from Broken Hill. He had a passenger in the car who said she saw Lasonya sitting with a man on a public park bench on the local rugby league oval, home to the Wilcannia Boomerangs.

The oval and surrounding area are fenced off, but the gates are always open. Locals often go to the oval to hang out after dark to drink in groups when the pubs shut their doors.

The woman was the only person Keith spoke to who could say for sure that she had seen Lasonya alive on Saturday. That possible last sighting of Lasonya could have been a vital piece of evidence in the police investigation, and the woman told Keith that she had made a statement to police. As far as Keith knows, hers was the only sighting after Lasonya left Raelene and Katrina's grandmother's house at 6.30 pm on the Friday that was formally reported to the police. Keith still doesn't know whether police followed it up or investigated further at all.

Through his own efforts, Keith had pieced together a rough timeline of Lasonya's whereabouts over the weekend – but when he attempted to present the information he had gathered to the authorities, he says, they brushed it off as 'rumours'. He didn't feel like the authorities were listening to him. He speculated that this was because of his own police record: he had a long history of serious crime. 'I done thirty odd years in jail, you know,' he said.

Lasonya Dutton

Keith then heard something that piqued his interest: a neighbour had seen something unusual near Nanna Norm's house on the Monday at 11 pm, the night before Lasonya's body was found.

* * *

Ingrid Bugmy is a relative of Lasonya's and a friend of the Dutton family. She lived on Barkindji Drive, across the road from Nanna Norm's house. On the evening of Monday 28 March, she had been sitting on the front porch of her house chatting with a friend when something caught her eye in the darkness of night.

'I was sitting up here having a yarn, like a talk to one of my friends who was here, and I turned to the side and I looked over towards Aunty Norm's, where I saw at least one person standing outside the window,' Ingrid said.

'The light was on and I saw someone standing in the middle of the window. When I looked away and looked back again, they were gone.

'It looked to me like there were two figures standing there and one of them was holding up a phone light while the other tried to open the window.

'That was the night before her body was found.'

The window was Lasonya's bedroom window, and Ingrid had a clear line of sight to it from her front porch, about a hundred metres away. If what she remembered was correct, at least one of the figures she saw would have been standing no more than five to six metres away from where Lasonya's body was found.

At the time, Ingrid thought the scene was 'a bit odd'. But it wasn't until the next morning, when she awoke to a large police presence in and around Nanna Norm's home, that her mind began to tick over with fears about the two shadowy figures she believed she had seen the night before.

'It was strange for me to see someone standing outside of that window and then the next day they find her body there,' she said. 'They was standing there for a minute … probably a minute to two minutes, then they disappeared.'

Ingrid would later say it appeared as though the strange figures were attempting to jimmy the screen off Lasonya's window to gain access to her room.

When Keith heard about this, he put the word out and asked everyone in the family and those who regularly visited Nanna Norm's house if it was any one of them – but no one came forward.

Keith believed Ingrid's testimony could prove to be crucial to the investigation. But when he raised it with the police, he was told once again that people were just spreading 'rumours', and that it was not helping their investigation.

Keith found this immensely frustrating. He didn't see the information he'd gathered as just rumours. He said they might

Lasonya Dutton

have been 'yarns' to police, 'but yarns get convictions, you know.'

You've got to ask questions, Keith said, and talk to the right people. 'You gotta ask people you know … and then people who walk around talking and saying yarns and spreading yarns. They are the people you gotta go see and ask.'

Keith had a theory about what might have happened to his daughter. The theory involved a baby stroller and a laneway, half-a-kilometre long, that led right to Nanna Norm's backyard, away from the view of prying eyes on the road, allowing access with minimal risk of being spotted. Keith believed this laneway could have been used to transport his daughter's body. He had heard that someone was seen pushing a pram around the area before her remains had been discovered. The two shadowy figures the neighbour had seen at the window were, he thought, attempting to place Lasonya's body inside the house. When they couldn't get in the window, they had put her body in the backyard instead, and tried to make it look like a suicide.

This theory has never been explored by police, and no evidence has been presented to suggest it could be possible. However, the idea played on Keith's mind. This might be because he, like others involved in the *Dying Rose* podcast, did not believe police had done enough to look into the shocking circumstances of his daughter's death in the early days of their investigation.

Keith said that he had often seen a person pushing a baby stroller around the town, using it to transport alcohol cartons and items from the local grocery store. It was odd, yes. But what made it more so was the fact that Keith didn't see the stroller again in the weeks and months to come.

* * *

Among the NSW Police detectives interviewing people in the Mallee was a female officer who returned to the Dutton house three days after Lasonya's body was found.

When she was discovered, Lasonya had been wearing a grey hooded jumper and black Puma tracksuit pants with a white stripe. Wrapped around her neck was a black Xbox 360 audiovisual cord, the kind gamers use to connect their console to a television. The electrical cord was 180 centimetres long, and Lasonya's body was about two metres from a fence post.

Keith said he remembered the female detective taking out an Xbox 360 cord – he didn't know if it was the actual cord or just an identical one – and tying it around the top of the fence post, then stretching it out to where Lasonya was found.

It didn't reach.

Keith saw what the detective was doing and looked at her in disbelief. 'I just looked at her and said, "You gotta be kidding, right? My daughter wouldn't go out like that."'

Lasonya Dutton

Suicide wasn't a possibility he had even considered – he knew Lasonya, and she would never have harmed herself.

'She looked back at me and said, "Well, it's a theory we have, and we're looking into it."'

From that moment, Keith believed, just three days after his daughter's death, the police began treating Lasonya's case as a suicide – without first ruling out the possibility that someone else had been involved.

Keith argued the point, as any father would, telling the detective she was wrong – but that was it. The police packed up their equipment, told Keith they'd be in contact, and then, like the suspicious figure Ingrid saw standing at Lasonya's window on the night before her body was found, they vanished.

* * *

Keith said the local police came by the house twice in the next few months. He had always felt that policing in Wilcannia was about controlling the way the Indigenous community lived, rather than working with them to achieve a functioning relationship, yet he felt hopeful after the first visit, which came just a week after detectives and crime scene investigators had packed their gear up and left. Still coming to terms with what had happened, Keith was sitting at home when the local police stopped by to check in on him, 'just to see how he was going'.

When they came by that first time, he said he felt they might genuinely be interested in helping him and his family figure out what had happened to Lasonya, but he soon began to doubt it.

Keith didn't hear from the local police or detectives for at least a month after that. Their second visit only came days after Douglas Smith and his former colleague at National Indigenous Television (NITV), Dijana Damjanovic, had started making inquiries about Lasonya's death.

Keith was still running his own investigation and had gone to the media, reaching out to 'anyone and everyone', as he puts it, but only a few took the time to listen. Among them were Douglas and Dijana, who met up in Broken Hill in early June and drove out to Wilcannia together to visit the Duttons at their home. Keith took them into the backyard and they stood where Lasonya's body was found as he pointed at the kitchen window. They were both shocked to realise just how close Lasonya had been to the house, and how easy it would have been for anyone coming in and out the back door or looking out the kitchen window to see her.

Keith told them that the house was 'like a drop-in centre', with people going in and out all the time. Other family members backed him up: 'With the amount of people that go to Nanna Norm's house on a daily basis, I don't understand how she could have been missed,' Lasonya's cousin Katrina said. 'Like, there are always people going

Lasonya Dutton

through there throughout the day. How could they not have seen her?'

Douglas and Dijana stayed for a week, working on Lasonya's story. They put multiple questions to the Wilcannia police, and also to NSW Police headquarters in Sydney, asking what they were doing to find out how Lasonya Dutton had died, and if they could interview them. They were met with a wall of silence. The local police declined to speak on the record about anything to do with Lasonya's case and instead referred them to the lead investigator's office, which also refused to comment.

All they received was this statement:

Officers from Barrier Police District commenced an investigation into the death of a 31-year-old woman on Tuesday 29 March 2022 under Strike Force Moay.

The investigation has explored various lines of inquiry regarding the circumstances of the woman's death, which will be included in the report to the Coroner.

Since the beginning of the investigation, there has been significant engagement between local police, including Aboriginal Community Liaison Officers, the woman's family and those affected in the community, including updates on the investigation, ongoing support and welfare checks.

When the local police made their second visit to Nanna Norm's 'just to see how he was going', it felt to Keith like they were only there because the media had started taking an interest in his daughter's story. The police wanted to be able to say they'd checked in with the Duttons recently – and perhaps find out what Keith had been telling journalists.

'To me, it's like they're worried about what I'm doing, what I've got going on in my head, what I'm gonna do,' Keith said. 'It feels like they don't do the job they're supposed to do out here. It's out of sight, out of mind.'

Douglas and Dijana did a news story for NITV and also a digital piece for the channel's website, reporting that Lasonya's family were calling for a coronial inquest into her death. The headline was '"Horrified": Wilcannia family searching for answers following young woman's death'. They quoted Keith, saying that he was appalled by the way his family had been treated by Wilcannia police, and that the official investigation had 'returned absolutely nothing'. He described his anger and frustration, saying that everyone around him knew he was 'a time bomb waiting to explode'.

The piece was widely read, but no one else in the media picked up the story. It was the first and only article that went out on Lasonya Dutton's death that year. 'We didn't get a single phone call about it,' Douglas said. If this had been a 31-year-old white woman from an affluent area, Dijana wondered, how would the media have treated the story?

114

Only a few weeks later, Douglas received a call from a former colleague, telling him that Gemma Jones, the editor of the *Advertiser*, wanted to talk to him about a job. They met for coffee and Douglas told Gemma about the trip to Wilcannia and the Barkindji woman found dead in her backyard in plain sight. They talked about him coming to the *Advertiser* and continuing to work on Lasonya Dutton's story. Douglas resigned from NITV and joined the *Dying Rose* team in Adelaide in July 2022.

As 2023 began, Keith was no closer to the truth about how his daughter had died, but he still refused to believe that her death had been a suicide and wanted to see the responsible person brought to justice.

In the first months of the year, there were a few new developments.

After months of planning by the *Dying Rose* team, Douglas was about to return to Wilcannia, just a few days shy of the anniversary of Lasonya's death. He would spend time with the family and help Keith pursue the answers to his questions.

In preparation for his trip, Douglas went back to the NSW Police and told them he was working on a podcast that would look into the lives and deaths of six Indigenous women, including that of Lasonya Dutton. He explained that Lasonya's family were concerned that police had not taken enough statements from witnesses, nor adequately investigated the circumstances surrounding her death. 'They still have questions,' he wrote in his email.

Douglas also asked what the current status of the investigation was and requested an interview with the detectives in charge. His request for an interview was denied. Instead, the police media unit sent back exactly the same statement, word for word, that they had sent in June 2022.

Following their response, Douglas went back to the NSW Police a third time. He outlined a number of assertions made by the Dutton family: that detectives had taken no formal statement from Merle; that police had not continued to engage or communicate with the family after they packed up the crime scene; and that multiple witnesses had seen Lasonya in the company of a man known to her late on the Friday evening but no further investigation or inquiries had been made after the police left Wilcannia.

Again, the police automatically sent back the exact same statement and refused to directly address any of the assertions made by the Dutton family. Neither Keith nor Douglas had expected that police would actually address the assertions individually, but they had hoped that they might provide a more extended response, letting the family know that they were still looking into Lasonya's death. It never came.

In late February, a few weeks before Douglas was due to arrive, Keith finally received a copy of Lasonya's autopsy report. It was thirteen pages long, dated 10 February 2023, and arrived in the mail. The report confirmed that Lasonya had probably died on Saturday 26 March 2022 and said that her

Lasonya Dutton

body had been in an 'advanced state of decomposition' when it was found. It quoted police as stating that Lasonya's death was suspicious and that they had treated it as such, conducting a 'thorough investigation'. The police were unsure whether the position Lasonya's body was found in had been caused 'by a third party or secondary to postmortem predation', the report's author said, but they had ultimately determined her cause of death to be suicide – *despite being unable to rule out third-party involvement.* The report's conclusion was that, contrary to the view of the police who had investigated, the cause of Lasonya's death was 'unascertained'.

With the autopsy report finally in his hands, Keith finally had something that told him he wasn't crazy – that he wasn't making some far-fetched story up in his head after listening to all the rumours going around town. The report told him what he and his family had suspected ever since Lasonya's body had been found: that her death *had* appeared suspicious. There it was, printed in black and white: police had initially believed it too. There was a possibility someone could have been responsible for his daughter's death, *and they hadn't yet ruled out that possibility.*

If there *had* been another person involved, they could still be walking around the community – in fact they'd been walking around free for the past twelve months – so something should be done about it. Keith wanted justice for his daughter.

After he received the autopsy report, no NSW Police representatives came to see him. There was no phone call from the detectives who had investigated Lasonya's death. In fact, there was no contact from the NSW Police at all. After almost a year of silence from the authorities, he felt like they had abandoned the investigation and there was nothing more they were going to do.

It was unlikely much could be done at that point: over the course of twelve months, witnesses' memories would have faded, and if there had been any physical evidence that the police hadn't found when they walked the Mallee and made inquiries shortly after Lasonya's death, there was a good chance it wasn't there anymore.

But the autopsy report felt like something fresh, something new to work with. Keith wanted to make sure that the police had seen it too. He thought he'd better take action and go directly to them. He was sick of sitting around and waiting for them to come to him. He and Douglas agreed that they would go together to speak to the police when Douglas arrived in Wilcannia. To Douglas, it felt like Keith had been left to solve his daughter's death by himself.

Not long after Keith received the report, he also received an unexpected phone call from the New South Wales coroner's court. He felt a sense of hope, hearing the voice of a young Aboriginal woman on the other end of the phone.

Lasonya Dutton

The young woman was the newly appointed Aboriginal coronial information and support program officer at the coroner's court, and her job was to help Indigenous people overcome the barriers they face in dealing with the coronial system after losing a loved one. She was the first person to hold that role in the history of the New South Wales coroner's court or at any coroner's court in Australia – even though the creation of such a position in every state and territory in Australia was a recommendation of the landmark 1991 Royal Commission into Aboriginal Deaths in Custody, more than thirty years earlier.

She had also received Lasonya's autopsy report and was shocked at what she was reading. She told Keith that the state coroner was looking into the gaps in the NSW Police investigation into Lasonya's death. She also said that she was going to make the trip from her office in Sydney to Wilcannia to speak to Keith and the rest of the Dutton family in person.

* * *

In mid-March, on the second day Douglas was back in Wilcannia, he went around to Nanna Norm's to collect Keith and take him to the police station. When he arrived, there was a bit of a commotion in the front yard. The night before, an arrest had been made. Keith's niece, a girl barely eighteen years old, had been locked up by the local police over an incident at the hospital. She was badly bruised and a bit beaten up, and phone footage showed a young male police officer grabbing her roughly and pinning her to the ground to throw handcuffs on her.

It wasn't very clear from the phone camera footage what had prompted the arrest, but the last thing you saw was the girl being thrown into the back of a paddy wagon before being whisked away.

Arrests happen quite often in Wilcannia, especially to those in the Aboriginal community. It's not unusual to see a person's family members growling at the police as officers handcuff their loved one in front of everybody – and that's what this footage showed.

As Douglas jumped out of the car at Nanna Norm's house, the older brother of the young girl who was arrested the night before was standing there, visibly agitated and upset.

His name was Reggie, and he wanted to know why the police had been so heavy-handed with his sister. So Keith, Douglas and Reggie all jumped in the car and headed down the main street to the local station, which sits adjacent to the court house.

When they got there, no one was around. The station looked closed and all of the police vehicles were gone. They got out of the car and walked to the front door, where Keith pushed a button on a little speaker box to talk to the nearest police station – two hours away in Broken Hill.

Lasonya Dutton

A woman's voice on the other end of the line told Keith that the local sergeant was on annual leave and that all the other officers were out of town until that afternoon, but then, as Keith, Douglas and Reggie turned around to walk back to the car, a police vehicle unexpectedly pulled into the yard. It was a Toyota LandCruiser with a paddy wagon at the back.

The three of them walked towards it, with Keith leading the way. He had Lasonya's autopsy report in his right hand and looked like he was ready to hand it over to someone, or read it aloud.

The passenger door of the police vehicle opened, and the same officer who had arrested Reggie's little sister the night before emerged. He immediately recognised Reggie as her older brother and took a step back, as though he was getting into a better position to protect himself. Reggie hadn't even spoken a word, but to Douglas it looked as if the officer already had it in his mind that this was an unfriendly visit. He knew why both Keith and Reggie were there. It wasn't for a chit-chat, it was for answers. Keith wanted them, and so did Reggie – but they hadn't approached the officer in a hostile way.

As Douglas stood back and observed, Keith began talking, asking if he could speak to the sergeant and whether the station had received a copy of the report.

The young officer told Keith that the sergeant wouldn't be back for a few days and that they didn't know anything about the autopsy, just as Keith had suspected. Keith told the officer he should take a copy of the report and pass it on to the sergeant.

Keith then told the officer what was in the report, and he looked shocked. Keith said he wanted to speak about everything that was in there and especially the part about the 'thorough investigation' into Lasonya's death. He told the officer that the coroner had come back after twelve months saying that Lasonya's cause of death was 'unascertained'.

The officer said he'd pass the message on to the sergeant.

Reggie then asked something along the lines of: 'So what happened to my little sister last night, eh? Why'd you have to get rough with her and arrest her like that? She's only little.'

The atmosphere was tense and Douglas could see an argument was starting to brew. Reggie and the officer exchanged a few more unpleasant words before Keith told Reggie to wrap it up. The three of them retreated back to the car and the officer went inside with his partner.

To Douglas, it seemed like that was the way the police and the Aboriginal community in Wilcannia interacted with each other on a daily basis: the community indignant, angry or aggrieved, the police hostile and defensive.

* * *

'Me and my family still believe that she was murdered,' Keith told Douglas back at Nanna Norm's.

In the year since she had died, there had been no evidence that Lasonya met with foul play. But given no formal statement was taken from Merle – the person who stumbled upon her dead body – Keith believed there were still questions to be answered.

Douglas spent the week in Wilcannia, retracing Lasonya's last steps on the weekend she went missing.

He sat down with Raelene and Katrina to go over the last day Lasonya spent with them and to find out if they had given a formal statement to detectives. Raelene said she remembered speaking to a detective and that they'd had a recording device going as they spoke. However, Katrina wasn't sure if they were recording or if they had written anything down.

'They came and asked me a couple of questions, but that was it. I don't even remember them writing anything down … they just asked how she was that day,' Katrina said. Both Raelene and Katrina said they only spoke to the detectives for 'five or ten minutes'. The two cousins said they had described the last day they'd all spent together and mentioned that Lasonya had walked off at about 6.30 pm. Both women told Douglas that they were not confident that the two detectives had taken enough detail from them, and that the 'interview' was more or less a quick stop by for a chat.

* * *

DYING ROSE

It turned out that the state coroner could also see that something was amiss.

When the Aboriginal support officer from the coroner's office arrived in Wilcannia in mid-March, Douglas had already been there for a week with Keith and his family, who were patiently awaiting her arrival. He didn't know what information the young woman was coming with, but he knew it had to be something significant.

Most of the Dutton family were at Nanna Norm's house that day. It wasn't just Keith waiting for answers – it was clear how eager everyone was to hear what this young woman had to say.

Before she arrived, Douglas had asked for permission to record what she was going to tell Keith and his family, but it was denied. Douglas was told that the court was now looking to establish an inquest into Lasonya's death and the police investigation that had followed. Douglas was allowed to sit and listen to what she had to say, but not to record it.

Keith started by telling the young woman about Lasonya and where she had been found. He spoke about how she'd left Raelene and Katrina's house on the Friday and was supposedly seen a few more times after that.

He also mentioned who she was seen with and what he believed was the last known sighting of Lasonya alive, at 2 am on Saturday morning, when she was seen by a passenger in a car driving into Wilcannia from Broken Hill.

Lasonya Dutton

When Keith started speaking about the police investigation, the look on the officer's face started to turn. It wasn't a look of surprise, Douglas says, but a look that said she understood the Duttons and their concerns.

After about an hour sitting and hearing from the Dutton family, the young woman from the coroner's office asked if they would show her the backyard, so she could see where Lasonya's body was found.

Keith stood up and told her to follow him. Douglas followed too, hanging back and watching as they walked around the side of the house and into the yard.

When Keith pointed to where Lasonya had been found, the woman's face dropped. She was gobsmacked, just like Douglas and Dijana had been.

The woman was not a detective, nor was she qualified to investigate deaths, but it was obvious that she saw immediately why the family found it hard to believe Lasonya had taken her own life. It seemed too great a stretch – not just the distance, but also the logic.

Before she left, the young woman told the Dutton family that the coroner's court was now working towards a potential inquest into Lasonya's death, and asked if they wanted it to be held in Wilcannia or Sydney. Naturally, Keith wanted it at home, in Wilcannia – where Lasonya had taken her last breath, and where the whole community could be there to find out what more there was to know about what had happened to her.

125

After the young woman's visit to the Dutton family, Keith said he felt a sense of relief. Like the ball had finally landed in his court.

* * *

As this book goes to print, the potential coronial inquest into Lasonya Dutton's death is yet to take place. It is impossible at this point to predict what, if anything, it may uncover, and if it will provide the answers the family is looking for. It is, however, possible to predict some of the questions that may be asked, particularly about the alleged shortcomings of the police investigation. Douglas discussed what these questions might be with former NSW Police homicide detective Gary Jubelin.

Gary Jubelin first became involved in the *Dying Rose* podcast after hearing about it from producer Dan Box. Gary and Dan had both investigated the murder in the early 1990s of three children in the rural New South Wales town of Bowraville: Gary had been sent to re-investigate the case in 1997, after what was deemed to have been an inadequate response from NSW Police, and Dan had re-examined the murders for a podcast while working as a crime reporter for the *Australian* in 2016.

In researching the *Bowraville* podcast, Dan had spoken to Gary at length about the failings of the original police

126

Lasonya Dutton

investigation. They both saw parallels now with the investigation of Lasonya's death, and Dan had suggested that Gary should talk to Douglas.

Gary outlined the history of Bowraville murders for Douglas: between September 1990 and February 1991, three young Aboriginal victims – Colleen Walker, sixteen, Evelyn Greenup, four, and Clinton Speedy-Duroux, sixteen – had all gone missing from a part of Bowraville known as the Mission, after parties held there.

'Three children living in the same street disappeared in a small country town,' Gary said. 'It warranted homicide detectives leading the investigation, but the person that led the investigation in the early stages had never run a homicide before.'

This wasn't a criticism of the lead detective, he said, as he had been allocated to that position by people higher up. It was just one indication that the investigation wasn't given the priority it should have been.

'I honestly believe, and I've said this publicly, if the response was proportionate to what the crime was, the results could [have been] vastly different,' Gary said. He told Douglas that assumptions were made and investigative opportunities missed.

When the first child, sixteen-year-old Colleen Walker, disappeared, local police told her mother she had probably just 'gone walkabout' and didn't take a statement. That was two-

and-a-half weeks before four-year-old Evelyn disappeared, snatched from her grandmother's house sometime during the night after her mother put her to bed.

Gary said that if Colleen's disappearance had met with a 'proper response', and not treated as 'just an Aboriginal kid that might've wandered off and will turn up somewhere', there was a chance Evelyn might not have been murdered. 'If the police came into town and treated Colleen's disappearance as a murder right from the start, and flooded the town the way it would've happened if it was a white sixteen-year-old girl that disappeared on the North Shore of Sydney, it perhaps wouldn't have happened.'

But it did happen, and Gary said that the failure of the police investigation in its early stages likely led to one more death: that of sixteen-year-old Clinton Speedy-Duroux.

Like Colleen and Evelyn, Clinton also disappeared after a party at the Mission. His body was found in nearby scrublands, as was Evelyn's. Both had suffered trauma to the head. Colleen's body was never found, but her clothes were later discovered, weighed down with rocks in the Nambucca River. The New South Wales coroner ruled in 2004 that she had died and was most likely murdered.

Just as police had failed to properly respond to the murders, the media response also fell short: there was little-to-no coverage of the three disappearances at the time they occurred or after Evelyn and Clinton's bodies were found.

128

Lasonya Dutton

A suspect had been charged with the murders of Clinton and Evelyn in 1993, but when a jury found him not guilty of Clinton's murder, his trial for Evelyn's murder was abandoned. In 2005, he did eventually stand trial for Evelyn's murder and was again found not guilty. Subsequent applications to have the cases reheard at a joint trial have been rejected, and no one has ever been charged with Colleen's murder. For the families, the children's deaths remain an open wound, three decades on.

Gary saw many similarities in Lasonya's case. One of the first things he commented on was the decision by police officers at the scene not to take a statement from Merle Dutton, describing it as a failure of the investigation. After Merle discovered Lasonya's body, he should have been treated as a 'person of interest' until it was ascertained that he was only a witness and not a suspect.

'The person that's found the body would be a suspect in my opinion to start with, and you're clearly going to have to dissect the information that that person has,' he said. 'Any investigation I've run ... that's crucial. I can't see how you could say that the matter has been thoroughly investigated if you haven't spoken to the person that has found the body.'

Gary said that if the investigation were thorough, detectives would have asked Merle a list of questions intended to rule out his involvement in Lasonya's death.

As a former homicide detective, Gary said, his mind would have been ticking over with questions in the same situation, like 'What were you doing there?' and 'Why were you in the backyard at the time?' He'd have wanted to know when Merle last saw Sonya before finding her body, and how he'd come to find it.

To be clear, there is no suggestion that Merle had anything to do with Lasonya's death. What Gary was suggesting is that good police work is about ruling out potential suspects, and no effort was made even to talk to Merle. The police got lucky in a way: the person who found Lasonya had absolutely nothing to do with her death, but that's something investigators should never just assume.

He also raised the fact that Wilcannia is known for the rough relationship between the Indigenous community there and the local police. He thought the history of animosity between the two groups might have played some part, as well as unconscious assumptions and racial bias on the part of the police.

In everyday policing, he explained, your own background and the background of the people you're dealing with often comes into play, whether you know it or not – and sometimes that determines just how much time and effort investigators put into their inquiries when someone goes missing or is found dead.

'It's like: "Well, it's a blackfella, how much effort are we gonna give to that?"'

He said he'd seen cases throughout his career in which police assumed early on, without the necessary evidence, that a person had died by suicide. Those cases often, though not always, involved Indigenous people. If police come across a case in which a person with dark skin appears to have taken their own life, or if they know for a fact that the deceased has Indigenous heritage, they may assume it's suicide without considering other possibilities. Gary said that sometimes the automatic response, whether police acknowledged it or not, was: 'Oh, well, it's just another blackfella that's hung themselves ...'

'I don't assume someone's committed suicide just because they're hanging,' Gary said. 'I don't assume someone has committed suicide because they're lying with a rifle beside them ... You've gotta get the evidence to support a theory ... or a case theory.'

As for the lack of interest from the media and the general public, Gary said, a victim or community's low socioeconomic status can also come into play there – and Wilcannia, like Bowraville, is home to many families, especially in the Indigenous community, who struggle to get by on a day-to-day basis.

'If the prime minister's daughter was found hanging from a tree, the response would be disproportionately different,' he said. People living in poverty do their best to champion their missing or murdered loved ones, but they don't 'carry the power and the weight like connected people who get money behind it' and their cases don't get a lot of publicity 'because people just aren't interested'.

'Because it's an Indigenous community, it doesn't really impact them,' Gary said.

Public pressure, as a result of media reporting, can bring more resources to an investigation. When Lasonya died, NITV was the only media outlet that reported on the story. At the time, Douglas and Dijana thought the story would get much more attention than it did. But after it went to air and was published online, it was as if crickets were chirping. The Dutton family received no more media interest from anywhere – not until Lasonya's story was told by the *Dying Rose* team.

But perhaps the biggest similarity between the Bowraville children's case and Lasonya's was the failure of the police to communicate effectively with the families.

'If the family hasn't got the confidence that a thorough investigation was done,' Gary said, 'then that's damaging. Now, whether it was something sinister like murder, or whether it was a suicide, the fact that the family don't have the confidence in the investigation is concerning in itself.'

Douglas told him that the police had been at the Duttons' house for three days and then only contacted the family twice in the next twelve months.

Lasonya Dutton

'It doesn't cost anything to keep the family informed,' Gary said. 'I think that's a failing in policing ... It's a simple and humane thing to keep the families informed. Their loved one is dead. It doesn't take much to pick up the phone and go, "This is what we're doing, just to let you know."'

Whether Lasonya took her own life or not, detectives keeping the family informed could have eased their grief.

He said families often come to terms with the fact that their loved one has taken their own life if the investigators lay out all the facts for them.

'I've been involved in matters where it clearly is a suicide but the family won't accept it, so I've seen both sides and I'm not going into this naively,' Gary said. 'But the facts have got to support the findings ... that's important. The thoroughness of the investigation has got to represent the seriousness of what the investigation is. You're investigating the loss of someone's life and it does damage if it is not done properly.'

He added, 'You might find that when the inquest comes down it might've been a thorough investigation, but it doesn't matter if the families haven't been informed and kept apprised of the situation. The damage is still there.'

* * *

Following the release of Lasonya Dutton's episode on the *Dying Rose* podcast in September 2023, the New South Wales coroner's court subpoenaed all the material that Douglas had gathered in Wilcannia. That included all the documents he'd found, the footage he'd shot and the interviews he'd conducted over the course of more than a year, and all the correspondence he'd had with Keith and other people in Wilcannia such as Raelene, Katrina and Ingrid.

To the Dutton family, it felt like someone was finally taking them seriously.

LYLA NETTLE

Bolivar is the kind of place you drive past without really noticing. Home to just 357 people, it stretches along the western side of Port Wakefield Road about half an hour north of the Adelaide CBD. Every day, thousands of cars and trucks pass through on their way to or from South Australia's regional centres, or the Stuart Highway and then Alice Springs or Darwin. Very few stop.

But on the northbound side of the highway, a couple of hundred metres past one of Bolivar's petrol stations, there is a gravel parking area. It's full of potholes, surrounded by overgrown weeds and litter and offers nothing by way of facilities. Unless you're looking for it, it's easy to miss. The gravelled area is long enough for a truck to pull in for a rest or some urgent maintenance before heading back on its way. It has also become known as a free local camping site, where cars and caravans come to stay the night, or maybe longer. Between the camping site and the petrol station there is a wide ditch, actually a dry creek bed, its grassy banks lined by low, scrubby trees.

As the sun rose on Friday 17 May 2019, a mild morning for that time of year, a man we'll call Jason got out of a battered station wagon parked at the camping site and went to relieve himself among the weeds.

That, Jason later told police, was when he first spotted his partner, Lyla Nettle, lying on the steeply sloped embankment at the side of the road, just out of view of the cars and trucks whirring by. She was stretched out on her stomach, he said, beneath a small tree, and looked like she was speaking on the phone. He called out to her, but she didn't move, so he approached her and grabbed her – only to find her body stiff and her dark eyes grey.

Jason said he knew she was dead, but he tried to flag down a car anyway, before running to the petrol station and asking the attendant to call an ambulance. Paramedics were at the scene within minutes, but nothing could be done. Lyla was gone.

* * *

That lonely scene has played out in the mind of Lyla's mother, Susan Nowland, again and again since that day. It is not the overgrown weeds or the rubbish or the potholes that she gets stuck on – though it is painful to think that bleak car park is the last place that Lyla was alive. Instead, it is the near-unfathomable position her daughter's body was found in that morning that Sue can't stop thinking about.

Lyla Nettle

Lyla had been lying on her stomach, her head near the small tree and her legs stretched out down the embankment behind her, her feet pointing towards the dry creek bed just below. She had one end of a bungee cord tied around her neck; the other end was tied to an overhead branch, lifting her upper body up off the ground.

Her right arm was slightly outstretched, her hand touching the ground, and her left arm was tucked under her body. Police found foliage in her clenched left hand.

She was just five metres from the station wagon where Jason had spent the night.

Information released to the media by SA Police that morning said they were called to the area at about 8.30 am after the body of a 39-year-old woman was discovered. At that point, they weren't sure what they were dealing with.

TV cameras followed soon after, and vision captured at the scene showed detectives, forensics officers and a pathologist surveying the area where Lyla's body was found. It was cordoned off with tape and officers in forensics jumpsuits were taking photos.

It was a dramatic scene for a roadside car park, but standard for a death that could be suspicious. Police were still describing the death as 'unexplained' that morning – it wasn't immediately clear whether it was a suicide they were looking at or if it might have been foul play.

DYING ROSE

* * *

It was Lyla's brother Thibul who saw detectives pull up outside their family home, just a few suburbs away in Adelaide's working-class outer north. He had been going out to get a feed, but he came back inside with them.

'Who are these people?' Sue asked her son.

'They're police,' Thibul said.

'We're just here in regards to your daughter, Lyla Nettle,' one of the officers explained.

'Oh yeah, what's she done? Is she in jail?' Sue joked.

They said, 'Well, sadly—'

When Sue first told Kathryn Bermingham from the *Dying Rose* team about that morning, several years later, her voice cracked when she arrived at this moment in the story – the moment everything changed.

She couldn't bring herself to repeat the officers' words, but the emotion on her face and in her voice made it clear what they'd said next.

They didn't stay long, and Sue didn't get much detail from them during that first visit about what had happened to Lyla. They were still investigating why she had been found dead on the side of a busy road by her partner.

* * *

Lyla Nettle

Sue and her daughter had always been close. Lyla was Sue's eldest, born in October 1979. They were a Noongar family: Lyla's ancestors were Whadjuk people, whose country centred around Perth, where she was born, and Bibbulmun people from the far south coast of Western Australia.

When Lyla was a baby, her parents had lived in a notorious public housing complex in Perth called Brownlie Towers. It was ten storeys high and, as Sue put it, 'for all poor people'. Life was not easy.

Sue said there was so much violence there that she and her partner had actually broken into a vacant house and stayed there for about three months, to get away from the towers.

As a kid, her daughter had been placid, quiet and observant, Sue said. She helped out her parents by looking after her younger siblings a lot, and she never complained. Thibul said his big sister Lyla had been 'like a second mum' to him, as well as his best friend.

'She took on a lot of responsibilities as she was growing up,' Sue told Kathryn. 'But yeah, she always had a smile on her face. She never spoke badly about anyone and was willing to help people.'

Lyla was named after Sue's mum, her Nana Lyla, but her nickname was Lullaby. It suited her: she was a gentle, calm and soothing presence, and she loved music.

As she got older, Lyla got into a bit of teenage trouble. But generally, Sue said, she was a pretty good kid.

'She finished Year 12 but didn't do the best,' Sue said. 'But she tried.'

By the time Lyla was a young adult, the family had moved from Perth to Adelaide. She was finding her feet in the world. She was fun and full of life. Lyla had her ups and downs, and she struggled with depression at times, but Sue said she never lost her kind heart or her cheeky smile.

In her twenties, Lyla met a long-term partner and set her mind to having children. She'd always wanted to be a mum. But it was difficult. She lost three babies before her daughter was born in 2008. She also had a son, born in 2011. Sue said Lyla adored her two kids and was the best mother she could be, given her circumstances.

At some point, Lyla had started using drugs, but not hard drugs at first. Thibul said they were still close. 'I just never judged her, you know, I just thought that was my sister and she was going through what she was going through and I was just here for her.'

Her relationship with the father of her children eventually broke down. When they separated, her kids went to live with their dad. Then, in early 2018, Lyla met Jason at a rodeo. She fell for him hard, and the two quickly moved in together.

Though Sue had liked him at first, maternal instinct took over and concern began to creep in. 'At first I thought he was nice, but there was just something eerie about him,' she said.

Jason was a long-term drug user, and while Lyla had used drugs in the past, Sue and other members of the family felt that things had escalated after they got together.

'She wasn't the same person on drugs, obviously,' Thibul said, but she was 'still his big sister', and he says they looked out for each other.

Lyla was always honest with her mum about what was going on in her life – even when she knew Sue would not approve – and she told her that Jason had convinced her to use methamphetamine, or meth, also known as ice, by telling her it would enhance their sex life. He had even persuaded her to let him inject her, she told Sue, because she was scared of needles.

Lyla craved love. She always had. She'd wanted it so badly that she'd do anything to hang on to it, no matter what it cost her. Sue was livid and sent Jason Facebook messages telling him to stay away from her daughter.

Lyla also told her sister that Jason had injected her with drugs. She said she felt it helped them to connect with each other.

As her relationship with Jason continued, Lyla became increasingly isolated from her family and friends.

'She was becoming withdrawn a lot more, stopped seeing the family,' Sue said. Half the family didn't like him, but Sue 'sort of put up with him, hoping things would get better'.

Sue recalled a time in August 2018 when Lyla had called her feeling dazed and woozy. She'd sounded completely out of it. Worried, Sue had called an ambulance for her daughter.

'They actually gave her something to calm her down. But then when we got to the hospital, she was just going down further,' Sue said.

She'd asked the nurse to check her daughter's arm.

'She had four needle marks. They actually said if I didn't bring her in, things could have got worse.'

Lyla was transferred to Woodleigh House, a mental health unit in Adelaide's north-eastern suburbs.

'They put her in there because they said it was attempted suicide,' Sue said. 'We said, "Well, no, it wasn't."'

Jason didn't even seem to care when Lyla was admitted, she said. 'He just took off. He sent a message saying, *Your daughter's going crazy*, and left.'

When Lyla was discharged, Sue hoped it might be the end of her relationship with him, but they were back together two days later.

Another time, Sue remembered Lyla talking about having another baby. Jason didn't like that, Sue said. He'd told Lyla, 'I've always got my things packed, ready to go.'

'Doesn't sound like he will stay around when there's trouble,' Sue told her daughter.

'And then after a few more months, I didn't get to see her,' Sue said. 'I tried hard, but it was like he was keeping her away from everyone.'

About six weeks before her death, Lyla and Jason were evicted from their home for failing to pay rent. Sue offered to set up a room for Lyla at her place. 'Then I find out she's living in a car with him,' she said. 'She just couldn't get away from him.'

Soon after, Sue and Lyla had another argument about her drug use. Their disagreements never lasted too long, but sometimes they didn't speak for a while, or they'd go a few weeks without seeing each other. Sue thought it wouldn't be long before they made up.

Around that same time, Lyla told her family she'd landed a job in Queensland, working in the mines. Her brother, Thibul, said it had been a hard few months but it seemed like things were finally on the up. Lyla was planning on moving alone, and she would need to stay clean, as mining company employees are regularly drug-tested. It seemed she was committed to improving her situation and wanted a fresh start. Her relationship with Jason, which had by all accounts become toxic, would finally be over.

Lyla began saying her goodbyes and making preparations for the move. 'She was excited to go,' Thibul said. 'It was all happy.'

Sue and Lyla still weren't speaking, but Sue was pleased that her daughter was ending things with Jason. For the first time in a while, she felt optimistic about Lyla's future.

When she was told Jason had found Lyla dead on the side of Port Wakefield Road, Sue was overcome by grief. It didn't seem real.

* * *

One of the people at the scene on the day Lyla died was a forensic pathologist, who had been asked by SA Police to attend. When he arrived, just after noon, Jason's station wagon was still there. There was also a pink camping chair and some cooking equipment just nearby.

By that point, the ligature had been removed from around Lyla's neck, and her body had been laid out on top of a body bag.

Lyla was wearing jeans with the left leg rolled up to the mid-calf, and blue and white trainers. She also had on a purple top and grey hoodie with a black waterproof jacket. In the pockets of the jacket, there were a set of earbuds, a lighter, a pair of gloves and a hand-rolled cigarette. A black baseball cap with a Jack Daniel's whiskey logo was on the ground just next to her body.

The pathologist noted a ligature mark on Lyla's neck where the bungee cord had been. Rigor mortis, the stiffening of the body after death, had set in, but temperature changes overnight and during the day meant that he could not pinpoint exactly when she had died.

When he had finished his work at the scene, Lyla's body was taken to the Forensic Science SA mortuary, in Adelaide, where a full postmortem would be conducted.

* * *

A few days later, police told Lyla's family that her death had been a suicide.

That didn't make sense to Sue. How could they know that already, when there were still so many questions to be asked?

If Lyla had taken her own life, what had happened in the lead-up? Did she have methamphetamine in her system? If she did, Sue felt sure that Jason must have injected her, as he had in the past, according to Lyla. Had it been enough to kill her? Or to drive her to kill herself?

Lyla's brother, Thibul, had concerns too.

When he was told Lyla's death was a suicide, he said he was 'in two minds'. He acknowledged his sister's history of mental health issues, but he thought her decision to move to Brisbane showed that she had turned a positive corner.

'Because she did try, she attempted previously,' he said, referring to suicide. 'But her state of mind, going to Brisbane, that kind of threw me off – I thought she would have been fine.'

But there were some things that didn't make sense, he said, like where his sister's body had been found, and the position it was in.

Thibul and his dad visited Bolivar to see for themselves where Lyla had died. They thought it might help them make sense of it all, but it only left them with more doubt.

Thibul was surprised when he saw the tree his sister had been found near. It didn't seem tall enough, or sturdy enough, for her to have hanged herself from. It was more like a bush than an actual tree, he said – no real trunk to speak of, just a collection of spindly branches jutting from the ground.

'I know she was skinny, but would it hold her body?' he said. 'It didn't make sense. Also, the rope or whatever was around her neck, it was only a flimsy little thing.'

The police explained that 'death by hanging' was the provisional cause of death. The interim death certificate would say, 'death by hanging pending investigation'. The full death certificate would only be available after the police and the state coroner had concluded their investigations and the coroner made a finding. That could take some time, the police said – perhaps up to six months.

But to Sue it seemed that the police had made their minds up already: Lyla had died by suicide. They were just waiting for the coroner to confirm it.

* * *

In the months following her daughter's death, Sue was despondent. The unbearable grief of a mother forced to

Lyla Nettle

bury her child followed her like a dark cloud. There was no reprieve.

But there was more to it than that. As time passed, Sue's doubts about what had happened to Lyla only grew – especially when she visited Bolivar herself.

Some of those doubts were about the investigation. At the site, Sue found a pair of Lyla's socks and didn't know what to make of that. Why were they lying there on the ground? How had the police missed them? Why hadn't they picked them up? How thorough could they have been, if they'd missed something like that?

Even more troubling, though, were the basic questions, the ones that would plague her for years.

Why would Lyla have ended her life *there*, she wanted to know – by the side of the road at that dingy car park?

It was also hard to understand how she had done it. Had she really hanged herself with an elasticated cord from that scrawny tree with its branches so low to the ground?

Her daughter's body had been found in such a strange position, too.

The idea that Lyla had died by suicide on the side of Port Wakefield Road just seemed more and more far-fetched.

After all, she was the adoring mother of two young children. She was close to her family. She'd been making plans for her future. And while Lyla had experienced mental

149

health issues in the past, it had been some time since she'd had any serious difficulties.

It all seemed so unexpected, so out of character.

Of course, these are sentiments police hear from many bereaved families. Grief is by nature complicated, but suicide adds another cruel dimension as those left behind wonder why their loved one chose to leave them. Denial is a natural response.

As South Australian police commissioner Grant Stevens would tell the *Advertiser* as we researched Lyla's story, 'Unfortunately, due to the nature of suicide, families are often left with unanswerable questions, which can make the reality of these circumstances difficult to understand or accept.'

But when Sue eventually contacted police, her biggest question was one they should have been able to answer: why were they so sure Lyla had killed herself? Nothing that Sue had seen or heard had provided her with any such assurance.

She went straight to the source, contacting the detective in charge of Lyla's case. She had his email address – and if anyone had the information she was looking for, surely it was him.

She was told that the coroner's report should be available soon, as the six-month anniversary of her daughter's death was approaching.

Then, around mid-September, Lyla's sister spoke with police. They asked her about Lyla's state of mind prior to her death and also mentioned that she'd had drugs in her system when she died.

Lyla Nettle

When Sue heard about this, she had even more questions, so she emailed the detective in charge of Lyla's case again.

Quotes from the emails that follow have sometimes been edited for legal reasons, but their substantive meaning remains the same.

On 13 October 2019, five months after Lyla's death, Sue wrote:

> It's been a number of weeks since I sent you an email and I know the six months is coming soon where the report needs to be written.

Sue said she knew police had spoken to Lyla's sister a few weeks ago and asked about Lyla's 'mindset' before she died. She said she had learned from Lyla's sister afterwards that Lyla had drugs in her system when she died. Sue wanted to know what the drugs were, and how they'd been administered. Lyla was scared of needles, she told police – so if it had been injected, someone else must have done it for her.

Could they tell where it was administered and if someone had given it to her, Sue asked.

She ended her email:

> Lyla would be forty years old next week.
> Yours sincerely,
> Susan Nowland

DYING ROSE

With some apprehension, she hit send. She hoped her plea for more information would be received sympathetically, as the cry of a mother desperate for answers. She held her breath … and heard nothing.

Days passed, then weeks. Sue wondered whether the police had even received her email.

On 3 December, she wrote to the detective to follow up, saying that she hoped he had received her earlier questions and the information she'd supplied, and to ask when she would receive the police report from him, and the autopsy report from the coroner.

It was disturbing for her, not knowing why her daughter had died, she wrote.

Six days later, she finally received a reply, having waited almost two months:

Good morning Susan,

I am really sorry that it has taken me so long to get back to you. I unfortunately injured myself at work back at the beginning of October and have been off work and then on very restricted duties.

I can confirm that the file, including all of the reports, has been forwarded to the coroner's office. I am unsure on the timescales that they have, but once the coroner has reached their verdict all of the information will then be released. They will also make contact with me and

Lyla Nettle

give me permission to release all of Lyla's property back to you.

With regard to the drugs in Lyla's system, it was methyl amphetamines and it appeared that they had been injected into her arm. You and [Lyla's sister] both advised that Jason was the most likely person to have injected her and that she would not have done so herself, however I could not prove on this occasion that this is what had happened. There was mention by [Lyla's sister] that Lyla wanted Jason to inject her as she felt that it helped them to connect with each other. In any case the methyl amphetamines were not the cause of her death but would no doubt [have] played some part in affecting her mindset.

I am hoping that the full report will be made available by the coroner very soon.

Many thanks.

The detective's response frustrated Sue. Lyla had told her that Jason was always the one who injected her. She wondered what lengths police had gone to to work out what had happened that night.

It was frustrating, too, that she'd had to wait so long for a reply. Sue had been off work herself since before Lyla died, due to a knee injury that had left her unable to do her job and struggling with depression. She knew that sometimes a person might not be capable of carrying out their usual duties – but shouldn't someone else have been monitoring the detective's emails while he was off work? Surely his cases couldn't have been put on hold until he returned?

On 28 December, she replied, thanking the detective for the update and asking further questions. She also provided information that she thought would help the police to establish what had happened.

For example, she had asked where the puncture wounds were on Lyla's body that indicated she had been injected with drugs. In his reply, the detective had told her only that it appeared the drugs had been injected into Lyla's arm. He hadn't specified which arm, so Sue asked him now, explaining that Lyla was right-handed. If the puncture wounds were inside her right elbow, Sue assumed, that would be proof that Lyla had not injected herself – meaning that someone else had been responsible.

Could they tell her if these questions were considered, she asked.

She also wanted to know if the police would interview Jason again, if the coroner found anything to question in the account he'd given to police of her daughter's last day.

She said it had taken a toll on her, not knowing all this.

Sue had spent nearly a year wondering what had happened to Lyla. She had asked specific questions and then followed up, but it felt like police weren't listening to what she had to say – either that or they just weren't that interested.

'Her life just didn't matter,' Sue said. She felt like the police had just thought: *Oh, here's another Aboriginal girl. Drugs.*

But she couldn't let it go. There was no way. And so, on 6 March 2020, she wrote to the detective again.

It's been a few months now, and ten months since Lyla's passing.

I appreciated your last message, but you never did answer the questions everyone has on their mind, especially me.

She explained that Lyla had sent a message – a happy, positive one – to a friend in the early hours of Tuesday morning. It said that everything was fine, and that she was going to see her dad in the morning to borrow some money. Didn't that prove that Lyla had been in a positive mood? That she'd been making plans for the next day?

Sue wanted to know the time of her daughter's death too. It wasn't the first time she'd asked about it.

'Last message 3.30 am, and dead by 8.30 am in a ditch,' she wrote. 'What was the time of her death, PLEASE?'

And if the coroner found that Lyla's death hadn't been suicide, she wanted to know, what would happen then? Would the police take a second look into Jason's actions and the information he had given them?

'Please, I'm requesting these questions are answered,' Sue wrote. She said that her community, and others too, including many non-Aboriginal people and even some from overseas, had seen her posts on social media and were asking if it was because Lyla was Aboriginal and a drug user 'that she doesn't deserve and we don't deserve to be told the answers to our questions'.

'Can I request your report to be emailed to me?' Sue asked.

She signed off with 'Hope to hear from you', but again, she heard nothing. It seemed there was nothing she could say to prompt the authorities to respond with any sense of urgency.

On 13 May, the detective apologised for the delay:

Sorry for not responding earlier, I have been off work following surgery.

I understand that you have a lot of questions that you want answering to help you find closure [after] Lyla's passing. Unfortunately, we have to wait for the coroner to assess the file and issue their final findings as to the cause of death to answer [your] questions. For me to answer these questions could be prejudicial to the coroner's investigation.

He ended by suggesting that she call the coroner's court to ask for an estimate of when the finding would be released.

Sue was angry. She had sent the police leads to consider, timelines that she'd constructed, but she felt as if they hadn't even attempted to follow up.

What the detective said about prejudicing the coroner's investigation was true. The state coroner's office doesn't usually release much information about how a person died or the circumstances surrounding their death until a finding has been made, and the police cannot release those details either. Doing so could compromise the investigation – and there is also the risk that providing incomplete information could mislead the deceased person's family, adding to their pain, grief and confusion.

What seems clear, though, is that the police had not explained this to Sue at the start – or, if they had, that they hadn't explained it clearly enough, or at a time when she or other members of the family were able to take it in.

It also appears that Sue had been told, or at least given the impression, that the coroner would make a finding within six months of her daughter's death. There is in fact no specified period within which a finding must be made, and the time taken to investigate cases can vary greatly. If Sue had known this, she might have felt less anxious when the first anniversary of Lyla's death passed without any sign of the report she had been promised – the one that she thought would give her all the answers.

On 18 June, she wrote to the coroner's court – not, as the detective had suggested, to ask when the coroner would make a finding, but because she wanted whoever it was investigating her daughter's death to consider important facts that she felt the police had overlooked or ignored.

'My name is Susan Louise Nowland,' she wrote, 'and my daughter was found deceased 17th May 2019 in grassland near the Caltex Petrol station on Port Wakefield Road.'

Sue explained that police believed Lyla had died by suicide, but that she and her family – and even strangers who knew about the case – believed there was more to it.

She gave the coroner the few details she had about Lyla's death, then set out a long list of questions, making it clear that she had doubts about Lyla's partner's account of what happened that night.

She wanted to know about the injuries Lyla had sustained, and why Jason hadn't taken the cord from around her neck when he found her and done CPR.

She also wanted to know why Jason had said Lyla looked as though she were on the phone when he found her. Sue's understanding was that both of Lyla's phones had been found in Jason's car, so how could he have thought she was on the phone?

And something else about the phones had been troubling her: if Lyla had walked off after an argument with Jason, why would she have left her phones behind? Wouldn't she have taken them with her?

Sue also noted that Jason was a regular drug user. The police hadn't stated if they had found any drug-related items in the car, which made Sue wonder if Jason had, as she put it, 'got rid of this evidence'.

One question she asked made her fears especially clear. She explained that when she had visited the site, she had found a pair of Lyla's socks and thought it was worrying that the police hadn't picked them up. 'Could it be possible that Lyla's strangulation was from someone using socks to cover their fingerprints?' she asked.

'I am sorry this is a strange letter,' she concluded, 'but there have been many unanswered questions that have left us feeling very uneasy.'

Sue had hoped for fresh eyes on her daughter's case. Maybe someone would even see it and think it was a case that should be heard at an inquest. But it was the same detective she'd been corresponding with all along who replied.

On 8 July 2020, he wrote:

I have been asked to make contact with you on behalf of the Coronial Investigation Section.

I understand that this is all still very sensitive for you and your family and hope that I can provide some closure.

The circumstances and physical evidence at the scene of Lyla's death did not point in any way to her death being caused by Jason or any other person.

Due to what he described as the 'unusual location and position' of Lyla's body, a police pathologist and officers from Forensic Response, the two highest specialist departments in the field in South Australia, had been called to the scene to determine whether, in their expert opinion, Lyla's death could be classed as suspicious. Having viewed the scene and externally examined Lyla's body, they had ruled out foul play and the possibility that anyone else had been involved in her death.

For example, the detective wrote:

There were no injuries to her body indicative of a struggle or fight and there were no signs on the ground of any struggles or fights.

To further rule out any foul play, the pathologist requested an urgent postmortem be conducted. This then provided further medical proof that there were no internal injuries consistent with Lyla being murdered.

The only marks on Lyla's neck were caused by the ligature around her neck and these were consistent with the cause of death. The fact that Jason did not remove the ligature from her neck actually allowed the attending pathologist and Forensic Response officers to conduct a

Lyla Nettle

more thorough and sterile investigation. Had the ligature been removed things may not have been so clear.

He noted particularly that there were no scuff marks or finger marks consistent with Lyla having been strangled by a person wearing socks on their hands.

When reviewing Lyla's medical history, she had a couple of other suicide attempts in the past which were not completed. I believe that [it] is highly probable that she did not intend to succeed on this occasion, but unfortunately she did. I believe that, like in the past, this incident was a result of her taking illicit substances and having relationship issues.

It could not be ruled out that Lyla took her illicit drugs when not in the presence of Jason. He claimed that he did not have any knowledge of her taking them. No needles or illicit drugs were located in the car. It is possible that Jason could have got rid of them, but from what we could ascertain, he went straight from Lyla to the service station. No needles were located in the vicinity of the grassland.

With regards to Lyla's property, I will organise the release once I have been notified by the coroner's department that they can be released.

Many thanks and I hope this answers some of your questions.

Take care.

Sue wasn't happy with this response. The detective had finally given her some answers – but only because the coroner's court had directed him to, and the answers he'd provided all supported the theory that Lyla had died by suicide. Sue did not accept that Lyla had tried to take her own life in the past, and she was still convinced there was more to it than a suicide attempt.

'I wrote and I wrote and I wrote. I kept saying: Please, could you follow this up? Could you do this? Have you considered this?' she said. 'I gave them so much information. And it was like: we've done it all, we've checked it all out, and unfortunately, yep, they put it down to suicide. They just kept saying no, look, we've done everything. She suicided. Your daughter suicided.'

Sue found one of the detective's statements particularly baffling.

'It could not be ruled out that Lyla took her illicit drugs when not in the presence of Jason,' the detective had written. 'He claimed that he did not have any knowledge of her taking them.'

Although his wording was slightly ambiguous, the detective was saying that Jason claimed he wasn't aware of Lyla taking any drugs *on the night she had died* – but Sue misunderstood him. She thought he was saying Jason claimed he wasn't aware of Lyla *ever* having taken drugs.

Sue was understandably incredulous. Lyla's drug use was no secret. Her whole family knew about it – but now Jason was claiming he had no knowledge of it? How could Lyla's partner – who had been living with her *in a car* – be unaware she'd been taking drugs? Drugs had played a huge role in both of their lives! How could police believe him?

Sue had had conversations with Jason on Facebook about his and Lyla's drug use. That was clear evidence that he knew Lyla took drugs, wasn't it? She could have proved it to police, she thought, if they would just listen!

It was a simple misunderstanding, and it could have been cleared up easily, if the detective had called Sue to speak with her, or come to see her in person – in other words, if the process had been designed to allow any kind of meaningful follow-up.

Instead, Sue was once again left feeling confused and angry, convinced that the police hadn't asked the right questions. It seemed to her that they just weren't interested in the truth.

* * *

At around the same time Sue received the detective's email, she also received a report detailing the results of the police investigation into Lyla's death. Sue initially assumed, incorrectly, that it was the coroner's report. She would later learn that it had in fact been written by the detective in charge of Lyla's case.

As of January 2025, that report is still, several years later, the only document Sue has been given explaining what happened.

Like all such reports, it was grim reading, and especially so for a grieving mother.

Its very first line read:

The deceased was a 39-year-old female whose history was unknown. It was reported that the deceased had been admitted to Woodleigh House between 09/08/2018 and 11/08/2018 with suicidal ideation.

The report noted Lyla's height and weight, and, as is standard, the weight of each of her organs, including her heart and brain.

There had apparently been multiple puncture wounds, likely caused by needles, on the inside of both of Lyla's elbows.

A blood sample taken on the day Lyla's body was found had given a methylamphetamine reading of one milligram per litre, which the report described as 'relatively high'.

The concentration of methylamphetamine in a person's body can change due to biological processes that happen after death, and there are other factors that combine to determine whether or not a specific dose is fatal for a specific individual. The report described the level of the drug in Lyla's blood as 'non-fatal', although it was high enough that in other cases it had actually been the cause of death.

Lyla Nettle

There were further references to Lyla's medical history, including her drug use and previous suicide attempts.

There was also an account of Lyla's last day. It said Jason had picked Lyla up from her dad's house on 16 May, the day before she was found dead. They went shopping and then had an argument before parking at an oval in a suburb called Parafield Gardens, about five kilometres south of Bolivar. Lyla left Jason and the car, and he then drove to the roadside car park, where he planned to spend the night.

He had parked the car and used camping equipment to cook dinner while drinking wine, and sent messages to Lyla to say she was welcome to join him.

She did join him, arriving just before sunset.

The report seemed to rely on Jason's version of events when it said that Lyla had 'appeared agitated' and that they had continued arguing. It said she then 'appeared to walk away and then return'.

If other witnesses' accounts or evidence from the scene, such as CCTV footage, had informed the report, they were not mentioned.

Between 7 and 8 pm, Jason had packed up the station wagon and got in the back to go to sleep, while Lyla remained outside. According to Jason, he got up once during the night to go to the toilet and did not see Lyla. He then went back to sleep in the car and did not wake up again until the morning, when he discovered her body, just five metres from the car where he had been sleeping.

The report said nothing more about the period from when Jason went to sleep until he found Lyla's body in the morning. It gave no indication of where Lyla was during that time, what she was doing or if she had spoken to anyone. There was no estimate of when she had died. If police do know more about what Lyla was doing that night, they have never told her mother about it.

For Sue, it was another kick in the guts. It seemed that her concerns, and her pleas for further investigation, had amounted to nothing. The report just reflected what the detective had told Sue over their months of correspondence: that Lyla had taken her own life and that Jason had slept through the whole thing.

Sue had been expecting answers from the coroner, but she only had more questions. What had Jason heard that night? Had Lyla tried to get in the car with him? What were her last words?

Ultimately, the report's author concluded:

Taking all the findings into consideration, in my opinion this lady has died as a result of hanging. The deceased is likely to have been influenced by methylamphetamine at the time of her death.

Lyla Nettle

It went on:

> There were no findings to positively indicate the
> involvement of another party in her death.

It seemed the postmortem examination could not exclude the possibility that another party had been involved but that their actions had left no discernible marks on Lyla's body.

That is not, it should be noted, a disclaimer automatically included in every autopsy report, and it left Sue confused. If the pathologist hadn't been able to rule out the involvement of another person, how had the police been able to?

And there was still the question of the methylamphetamine in Lyla's system. Sue felt sure she wouldn't have injected herself. If Lyla had been under the influence of ice at the time of her death, and if Jason had injected her with it, what did that mean?

Sue was also bothered by the emphasis the report put on Lyla's mental health. Sue didn't accept that Lyla had been experiencing suicidal ideation. But, even if she had been, her admission to Woodleigh House had been nine months before she died. A lot had happened since then. Lyla did have a history of mental health issues, but Sue felt the report placed too much significance on that as evidence that she had taken her life. In Sue's mind, there was no way her daughter would have chosen to die.

But throughout all this, there was something else on Sue's mind.

Lyla was Aboriginal. She'd faced racism throughout her life, and now Sue feared she had faced it in death.

'There's always going to be that racism.' It was about how police perceived Aboriginal people, she said. 'Especially Aboriginal women, they're lower grade. They're not worth anything. If she was white, it would have been a bigger thing. But being Aboriginal, being with drugs, they didn't care. No one seemed to care.'

On Monday 7 September 2020, Sue wrote to the detective in charge of Lyla's case again, to let him know how she felt after reading what she still assumed was the coroner's report.

> I was taken back that a lot of what you had told us
> was not in the report. I could write ten pages of the
> differences, but it is clear to all that police just viewed
> Lyla as a drug addict who had already tried suicide and
> was put into a mental facility.

She reiterated that she felt police should be asking further questions of Jason, and said that she, the rest of Lyla's family and their community were all 'very disappointed in the police system', which was, she said bitterly, 'always the same'.

Sue ended by saying that she wished to make an appointment to retrieve Lyla's phones from police storage.

Lyla Nettle

This time, the detective replied promptly. The next day, he wrote:

The report I have submitted, which I suspect is the one you have a copy of, is based purely on the facts that I have been able to establish. The coroner's report will take into consideration not only my findings but the findings of other specialists.

One thing I am extremely confident in saying is that the coroner will not issue a finding that Lyla died due to an overdose, as there was no medical, physical or opinion-based evidence to suggest that an overdose caused her death. The cause of death was by hanging, and again the physical evidence at the scene and the expert medical opinion of the pathologist who attended the scene and conducted the autopsy both state that there was no other person involved in Lyla's death.

Due to the unusual location of where she died, a Forensic Science South Australia pathologist, SAPOL Major Crime detectives, Forensic Response investigators, Crime Scene investigators, Northern District CIB investigators and Northern District patrols attended and conducted the investigation. She had the highest level of investigators in the state conducting the investigation to ensure that it was not a murder and from the investigations conducted everyone who attended was of the same opinion: that no other person had a hand in her death.

After establishing that her death was not suspicious, it was then my responsibility to try and establish why she died. This process involves not only speaking to family but speaking to mental health services, doctors and establishing her history of drug use. I have to disclose in my report Lyla's history of drug use and also her previous suicide attempts as it is my responsibility to collate that information for the coroner.

The community disappointment should not solely be aimed at the police: it is a coronial investigation process, which is state wide and has been used and tested for the past few decades.

I take a great deal of pride in my coronial investigations and I put more effort into them than any of my other investigations because I want to find answers for families and gain closure for them. I do my best to treat the families and the deceased respectfully and in a manner I would wish to be treated if it was me in mourning. I would not put any file forward if I did not think all avenues of investigation had been explored.

I am sorry that you do not feel that I have fully provided closure to you and your family but I can only work with the facts that are presented in front of me.

He also noted:

I have been in contact with the Coronial Investigation Section and they have advised that the Coroner still has not issued his final report so the mobile phones cannot be released at this time.

* * *

Lyla had two phones with her on the day before she died. Strangely, though, the postmortem report made no mention of them. The report only listed the things that were found on Lyla's body, and she didn't have either of the phones on her. Sue said they were both found in Jason's car. The report doesn't mention the car being searched, but it must have been, because police had told Sue that no needles or illicit drugs were found in it.

Sue was convinced that the phones held more information about what had happened to her daughter. After asking in early September 2020 to arrange to pick them up, she emailed the detective several times over the next few weeks to follow up, asking when the phones would be available for collection. The detective told her, every time, that the coroner was not finished with them.

On 19 November 2020, Sue tried again.

The detective responded ten days later.

Good morning Susan,

I hope you and your family are well.

Unfortunately they are still not permitted to be released.

I am going to set a reminder for a month's time and I will chase them again for you.

On 30 November, Sue followed up.

'Just a question,' she wrote. She wanted to know if the police or the coroner had the phones, and why they still needed them.

'If the report has been done by the coroner,' she asked, 'then what is the reason for keeping the phones? The case is closed.'

The detective responded, saying that the phones were in the police property store.

'The case is still open with the coroner,' he wrote, 'and as such exhibits cannot be returned until the case is closed. I will keep chasing this for you.'

SA Police would eventually tell the *Dying Rose* team that Lyla's case had been finalised when the coroner's findings were handed down on 12 November 2020. It is unclear why Sue's subsequent requests that the phones be returned to her, made on 19 November and 30 November of that year, were knocked back.

By the start of the new year, 2021, a weary Sue felt she had reached the end of the road. She had been through hell since that day police showed up on her doorstep and told her that her daughter was dead. It had changed everything. But it felt like the rest of the world had moved on pretty quickly. Too quickly.

Still grieving, and starting to feel that she might never get justice for Lyla, she just needed to get away from it all – far away. She decided to move from her home in the northern suburbs of Adelaide to a place she had always loved.

Before she left, she wrote to the detective again, on 7 January, to tell him that she was moving away and that she did not want Lyla's phones anymore. 'Could they please be destroyed?' she asked. 'Due to family and grief, I don't think I want any information from them.'

She told the detective she was leaving Adelaide and moving to Bali.

The detective responded two days later, saying that he was sorry to hear that she was having family worries and leaving Adelaide. He added:

I still think it will be a while before I get advice that the phones can be released so there is no need to make any firm decisions on them being destroyed as yet.

Will you be using this email account still when you move to Bali? If so I will keep you notified about when the phones are available for release.

DYING ROSE

* * *

On the eastern coast of Bali, there's a seaside town called Candidasa. It's about a two-hour drive from Denpasar airport and not as touristy as the island hot spots that welcome hundreds of thousands of Australian travellers each year, instead offering idyllic coastal scenery and intriguing cultural experiences. It's a place you might go if you were looking for a bit of peace.

And peace was exactly what Sue was looking for when she moved to Candidasa at the beginning of 2021.

'I was so depressed with life,' she later said. 'And I've always had a love for Bali. I'd come back once or twice a year for the last nine years.'

Sitting at home in Adelaide, harrowed by grief, still unable to work because of her knee injury, Sue had felt her mental health take a tragic turn.

'When I got my payout, I was just thinking: *What am I doing in Australia?* Because I honestly didn't want to live,' she said.

'So the WorkCover people, they said to me, "Where do you see yourself next year?" And I said, "I'm going to be dead, because I'm not living."

'And they said, "Well, what do you want to do?"

'I said, "Look, I want to go to Bali – I want to heal there with the spiritual healers and everything."

174

'So yeah, they had a meeting and agreed that I could come and live here.'

Sue bought a villa at a sprawling resort positioned right on the water. It's a small but comfortable place, filled with natural light. She can hear the ocean as she drifts off to sleep at night and, during the day, birds visit and chirp at her front door.

Her villa is one of the closest to the resort's large pool, where she swims regularly as a form of exercise and therapy. It's next to the restaurant, and to the bar area, which plays host to a local band several nights a week. She loves to go along for a drink and a dance. She counts locals and other long-term residents of the resort among her close friends. She knows the best massage place and best restaurant in town, and where to get fresh produce or medical treatment. Here, she has found a community. She has everything she needs.

It was Courtney Hunter-Hebberman who originally introduced Sue to the team. Courtney's daughter Rose and Lyla had died only about six months apart, and the two mothers had connected online. They had bonded over not only the unique grief of a parent who has lost a child, but also the feeling that police weren't listening. Each felt there was more to the story of her daughter's death. That shared experience gave them a sense of solidarity – they were a support for each other.

Courtney didn't think Sue would want to talk to a reporter. She'd gone overseas to find some refuge from what happened, and talking about it would just bring it all back up again. But Sue surprised her. She'd had plenty of time to think in Bali. Thoughts of Lyla's last day and the way police had responded to her death still occupied her mind. The authorities seemed to have closed the book on Lyla's case, and no amount of protest from Sue was going to change their minds – so in 2022, when we asked her to be part of the *Dying Rose* investigation, she didn't hesitate. She had nothing to lose, and it gave her hope that maybe, finally, she would find out more about Lyla's death.

It wasn't until October 2022, when we first contacted her, that Sue thought again about Lyla's phones, wondering what new information they might hold. She had told the detective in January 2021 to destroy them, but he'd told her there was no need to make any firm decisions at that point and that he'd keep her updated. She hadn't heard anything about it since then, so she emailed him again, for the first time since she'd left Australia, to ask him to return them.

The detective responded:

Following the direction I received from you on 7 January 2021, the phones and all other property held were destroyed on 19 May 2022.

Kind regards.

It was another brutal blow, just as she'd started to get back on her feet. Sue admitted she'd told the detective the phones

176

could be destroyed, but he had told her there was 'no need to make any firm decisions on them being destroyed as yet' and that he'd notify her when the phones were released.

She'd thought she hadn't trusted the police, but obviously she had: she'd taken the detective at his word.

Sue accepted her share of responsibility – but it was disappointing. Now she would never know what her daughter's last messages were, and whether they might have shed any light on her state of mind that night.

* * *

In December 2022, Kathryn travelled to Bali to meet Sue at her villa. Kathryn, Emily and Douglas had been working on Rose Hunter-Hebberman's story for months at that point, but when Kathryn got on that plane, it felt like a big moment in our investigation. We had really committed to doing this properly.

Sue had arranged for her driver to pick Kathryn up. Kathryn had never been to Bali before, and she was struck by how noisy – and vibrant – it was. It was such a far cry from where Sue came from in Adelaide. Cars, trucks and scooters – lots of scooters – whizzed by as the driver dropped Kathryn off on Candidasa's bustling main street, lined with shops and stalls. But inside the resort, just past reception, was a quiet, peaceful sanctuary.

Sue messaged her, asking to meet at the pool. When Kathryn found her, she was doing slow, steady laps. She had the pool to herself and invited Kathryn to join her. Kathryn was hesitant at first – they'd only just met, and she didn't want Sue to feel pressured to talk. 'But it was pretty hot,' she says, 'so I did end up getting in, and we kind of floated around for a couple of hours, talking.'

Afterwards, Sue invited Kathryn into her villa, which was small but clean and full of light, and close enough to the ocean that you could hear the waves crashing outside.

Sue told Kathryn that she felt Lyla's spirit was still with her. Lyla was everywhere in the villa: there were photos of her, framed, on the fridge and on the walls. Sue brought out some of her daughter's things to show Kathryn – things she'd brought with her to Bali to remind her of Lyla. She had Lyla's favourite jumper, for example – 'God, it hasn't been washed for four years,' Sue said – and a bottle of her perfume.

Having those things around her helped her cope, she said.

* * *

When Sue was ready, they sat down and Kathryn took out a tape recorder. Over the course of their two days together, Sue recounted everything she knew about what had happened on 17 May 2019.

Lyla Nettle

There were times when she grew emotional. Though more than four years had passed since that morning she first heard the news, her grief was still raw and she found it difficult to talk about what had happened. When she needed a break, they would stop.

In a way, Sue had become a detective: searching through old messages for any sign of what was to come, piecing together bits of information she'd heard here or there, asking her own questions of various people connected to Lyla and Jason, going back over emails and the coroner's report. But still, she explained, there were key parts of the story missing.

For Sue, it all boiled down to Jason – the last person who'd seen Lyla alive. They'd fought that night, as he admitted they often did. Jason told police he had gone to sleep before 8 pm and that Lyla was, at that point, outside the car. He slept for several hours before waking up and leaving the car briefly to urinate, but he did not see her. He then went back to sleep in the car and woke up in the morning to find her body lying just five metres away.

Sue didn't understand how Lyla could have taken her life right there, on the side of the road, so close to the car, yet so quietly that Jason heard nothing.

She told Kathryn about the messages Lyla had exchanged with her best friend that night. At around midnight, Lyla had messaged her friend, mentioning that she needed some money. The last message she'd sent was at 3.30 am, saying,

It's okay, I'm here with my man looking at the stars. I'll go see Dad tomorrow. It's all cool.

Sue wanted to know why Jason said he'd been sound asleep from 8 pm until after the sun had risen, when Lyla was saying they'd been awake and looking at the stars together at 3.30 am.

The police had told her that Jason was taken to hospital that morning and treated for shock. They had interviewed him, but she did not know what they had asked him, or if he had been drug-tested.

For her, knowing if he'd been 'full of ice' was an important question. 'When you're on ice, you don't sleep,' she said. She knew, because she'd seen Lyla when she was on it. 'Like he reckons he slept from eight o'clock through the whole night, except for one time getting out to go to the toilet. On ice they go all day, all night.'

There was so much Sue wanted to ask Jason herself, so many questions that would go forever unanswered.

Or so she thought.

* * *

When Kathryn returned home from Bali, she couldn't stop thinking about Lyla.

Not long after, Sue asked her for a favour. She had set up a memorial to Lyla by the side of Port Wakefield Road, where her body had been found, with flowers and photos, but none of the family would go there. They didn't want to go to the place where Lyla had died. Sue said the memorial hadn't been visited in a while, and she asked if Kathryn could go there to straighten it up.

Kathryn felt like it was the least she could do, after everything Sue had done to welcome her into her life and shared Lyla's story with her.

In Bolivar, Kathryn saw for herself where Lyla had died. The potholed car park was a bleak, hopeless place, still strewn with rubbish and overgrown with weeds, but there was one splash of colour: Lyla's roadside memorial. Against the fence were flowers, photos and trinkets, and above them the words *Lyla Nettle RIP*. The photos were a little faded, and parts of the memorial had been knocked over or damaged, but it told passers-by what Sue wanted them to know. She loved her daughter, and this dingy car park was where her daughter had died.

Kathryn did her best to tidy it up, straightening the photos and brushing off the dust and dirt of the road. Then she drove home to Adelaide, determined to help Sue find answers to her questions and hopefully bring her some peace.

There was someone else she needed to speak with.

* * *

Sue's interactions with police to this point had been futile. She had not given up – she would never give up – but she had come to the realisation that if she was ever to find answers to the questions that haunted her, they would need to come straight from Jason.

The *Dying Rose* team agreed. By this point in the investigation, we had run into roadblock after roadblock in our efforts to get information out of authorities. We had tried contacting the coroner's court and been told the documents it held relating to Lyla's death could not be released because the matter had not gone to inquest. The police hadn't been keen to talk to us either. Going direct to Jason seemed like a better approach.

Tracking him down, however, proved difficult. He had not lived, and was not living, an easily traceable life. He had a limited online presence, no job, owned no property and was not in the White Pages phonebook.

His official address was near Gawler, a town about fifty kilometres north of the Adelaide CBD. Kathryn, Emily and Douglas visited the house and spoke to a young man working on a car out the front who identified himself as Jason's nephew.

'He's not here at the moment,' he said. 'He kind of comes and goes.'

The man was unsure whether Jason had another place but agreed to pass on a note with the reporters' contact details to his mum, Jason's sister. It felt like a dead end.

We finally found him with a bit of guesswork and a bit of luck. There were several Facebook accounts in his name, so we picked the one that looked most likely to be current and sent a message.

Nine days passed and, though the message had been seen by whoever owned the account, there had been no reply.

So we sent a second message. This one included a series of claims we were hoping he'd respond to – some from Sue, some from the detective's emails and some from the autopsy report.

That was on 18 August 2023, the day we launched the podcast.

This time, the response was fast.

I've been dealing with this for a long time, everyone saying lies, he wrote. *Despite what everyone is saying, it's all wrong and made up.*

He said he had flashbacks all the time and wasn't coping very well.

I get that people are hurting and need someone to blame, and I take my part in this tragedy.

Maybe you should look into the people who are telling you these lies.

Kathryn told him about our investigation – how we were looking at the deaths of several Aboriginal women, trying to figure out what had happened to them and why the police responded as they did.

DYING ROSE

After a bit of back and forth over Facebook, Jason agreed to meet up with Kathryn at a nearby shopping centre. He said he would tell his side of the story in person – and he wanted to do it immediately. *I will give you the truth*, he said, *not some story to make me look good.*

* * *

Elizabeth City Centre is a hub in Adelaide's northern suburbs. As well as shops and eateries, it has a police station and court, a library, a health centre, a theatre and a Service SA centre. It's a place that's always busy. On this particular Thursday, the car park was bustling and there were people milling about outside, doing not much.

One of them was Jason, easily identifiable from the photos on his Facebook account. He had a weathered face and looked like he'd had a hard life. He was friendly enough, though, and, after some small talk about the Adelaide weather, said he had been waiting for an opportunity to speak about what had happened to Lyla. He'd wanted to approach her mum and dad after she died to tell them what had happened, but he wasn't sure they'd want to hear from him, under the circumstances. In a strange way, the interview was fortuitous. Finally, here was his chance to speak.

'Ever since it happened, I've wanted everyone to know,' he told Kathryn.

184

They sat down on a concrete bench and he told her about his relationship with Lyla, going right back to the beginning.

As Sue had said, he and Lyla had met one night at a rodeo at Clare – a winemaking and tourism region in South Australia's Mid North.

He'd been drunk at the time.

'She was a smiley, lovely, happy girl,' he recalled.

He said they'd spent the night together in her cabin, but he didn't stick around.

'When I left in the morning, I left early. I left my number on the door and just took off,' he said. 'A couple of weeks later she rang me … I went round and seen her.'

That was that. Nearly overnight, Lyla and Jason became a couple. They began living together and spending most of their time together.

'I used to say to Lyla, "Why are you interested in me? I'm just a drug addict. I've got nothing, I'm no one special,"' he said.

When Kathryn asked what their relationship was like, Jason said things between them were far from perfect – they'd argued a lot – but that he'd never laid a finger on Lyla. 'Never. If anyone touched her, I'd wreck them,' he said.

'We were planning on going to Queensland, starting new lives, getting clean,' he said. It wasn't Lyla moving on her own, like her mum had thought.

He said their relationship had been good at first but turned toxic. 'Because of the drugs,' he said.

'Lyla was using drugs before I came along – the only difference is she wasn't using drugs with a needle. She was smoking it and drinking it. Stupid me, not thinking clearly ...'

Jason paused, as if he could not bear the thought of what he was about to say. But it was clear what he was getting at.

'So you introduced her to the needle?' Kathryn asked.

'Yeah. Yeah, I did. I should have never done that, and I have to live with that for the rest of my life,' he said. 'It feels really horrible. Makes me feel really low, really terrible. If I loved her, I shouldn't have done that.'

He said he would 'swap with her in a heartbeat'.

'If I could swap with her I would. She's got two beautiful kids that need her.'

Jason said there were other people who had also injected Lyla with ice, but he didn't think he had ever seen her inject herself.

Asked whether he had injected her in the day leading up to her death, he said he could not remember.

'I would have that week, for sure,' he said. 'See, that makes me feel so bad, hey. But I can't take that back now.' He paused, then added, 'I didn't want her to die.'

The conversation seemed almost therapeutic for Jason, who frequently mentioned the guilt and remorse he lives with. Perhaps it was those feelings that had led him to this moment – sitting in a shopping centre car park, speaking with a stranger and owning up to his part in Lyla's drug use.

Lyla Nettle

Seagulls squawked around a nearby bin and a plane passed overhead as Jason recalled the night Lyla died.

'Well, we'd been arguing for a few days,' he said. 'And she just kept going and going – it was very draining, you know. I said to her, "I just need a break."'

Lyla spent some time at her dad's place that day before Jason picked her up later. They'd been at each other and had both needed some time to cool off. Their relationship was already volatile, and sometimes their drug use really didn't help.

They had been living in Jason's car at that point, as Sue had mentioned, but he said they didn't mind. He had done it before, so he had all the gear and knew what to do. He liked the sense of freedom.

He told Lyla that day, 'I'll go and cook us a nice meal – we'll camp out and go to sleep.'

'All was good,' he said. 'We went to the bottle-o, I bought a bottle of red wine … Chicken, roast veggies and everything. And I cooked this on the side of the road for her.'

But Lyla kept at him, he said. 'She couldn't stop, she couldn't stop. It just kept on coming. So I ended up just turning it all off, and I said, "I'm going to sleep, Lyla."'

The way Jason told the story made it sound as though he never bit back when Lyla was laying into him. It was a reminder that she was not here to tell her side of the story, that her version of what was said between them that night will never be known.

187

When he got in the car, he said, it was still daylight outside.

'She was outside the car, she was yelling and carrying on, and I said, "Just come and lie down, let's lie down and have a sleep."

'No, no, she wouldn't stop,' he said.

He said he heard her outside for a while, but then it went quiet. He wasn't worried by the silence.

'She has a friend that lives not far from there. So I thought, *Maybe she's walked off and gone to cool off with her.*'

He said as soon as he lay down, he was out cold. 'I passed out,' he said.

'I woke up during the night – I dunno, must have been one, two – I can't remember now. But I got up for a piss, I went for a piss and I looked down and her stuff's there. Her bag and a few things are next to the car. I thought that was a bit odd. I picked them up, put them in the car and, like I said, I thought she must have gone to her friend's. The last thing in my mind was *this.*'

So far Jason's story matched up with the version in the report the police sent to the coroner, which Sue had suspected was based largely on his word.

Kathryn asked him about the messages that Sue said Lyla had sent to a friend, including the one at 3.30 am saying, *I'm here with my man looking at the stars.* Kathryn hadn't been able to sight the messages – she had asked, but Sue said she'd lost touch with Lyla's friend – so she was curious to hear his response.

Lyla Nettle

'I don't know why she would say that,' Jason said. 'I don't, I find it odd.'

He says after he urinated, he got back in the car.

'I fell back asleep, woke up in the morning, it's daylight now. I get up, go for a piss again,' he said. 'I stepped out of the car, but, because it's daylight, I can't take a piss where I was last night, because everyone can see, cars are coming past. Luckily I walked over to the fence, took a piss, and then I just happened to look down and there she was on the ground. She wasn't hanging in a tree or nothing like that.' He held his hands out, palms up, and added, 'She was like this and laying flat.'

At first glance, he said, it looked as though Lyla was on her phone. But he quickly realised the gravity of the situation.

'I yelled and yelled, she didn't move. I raced down there, I grabbed her and she was so stiff, and I still have flashbacks of this,' he said. 'She just rolled over, and her grey eyes just looked at me right in the face. I knew she was dead at that point. I knew.'

He recalled running shirtless up Port Wakefield Road to the petrol station to ask the attendant to call police and an ambulance, which arrived quickly.

'They just sat me down behind the servo. I said, "My partner's over there and she's dead." They said, "We'll go and have a look." They went and had a look, they came back and said, "There's nothing we can do."'

The ambulance took Jason to hospital, where he spent two days receiving treatment for shock.

He said he was interviewed by police at the hospital and asked to provide details of where he had been that week. He said he hadn't been drug-tested in hospital, but that he had told the police he took drugs.

'I told them I was on drugs, straight up. I told them Lyla was. I said we both were. It's a well-known fact I'm a known drug user. It's no secret,' he said.

Kathryn told him about the ambiguously worded email Sue had received from the detective, the one that led her to believe Jason had claimed to have no idea that Lyla had ever taken drugs.

'I wouldn't have told the coppers that,' Jason said. He said he knew damn well that Lyla took drugs. 'Why would I say that?' he asked. 'It's a stupid thing to say.'

He said he was 'just thrown out' of hospital the next day. After that, he heard nothing.

He freely admitted that he had been expecting more scrutiny.

'I'm sitting there thinking, *What are they going to do?* You know when a partner, wife goes missing or dies, the cameras are there, and next thing you know, *this bloke's guilty,*' he said. 'That's what I was picturing. I was picturing I'm going to have cameras in my face in a minute. I didn't know. There were rumours going around, all over Facebook.'

190

Lyla Nettle

It was difficult to know how to read Jason. He seemed at pains to point out all the things he had done wrong. But he was adamant – he had never harmed Lyla and he certainly hadn't killed her.

So what did he think had happened to her?

'I honestly don't believe she wanted to kill herself – I just don't think she did. I choose to believe that she just was crying out for help,' he said. 'The way she was and that, it just looked to me like she thought I'd come rushing out, maybe, or someone. And I would have. I wish I knew, I really do. I get sick every time I go down Port Wakefield Road – I don't go down there anymore. I can't drive past there.'

Kathryn said, 'I know this is a really hard question, and I'm not suggesting that you were directly responsible for the death, but afterwards, given everything that happened, did you feel in any way responsible?'

Jason seemed almost annoyed, as though the answer should have been obvious by that point. 'Course I do, course I do,' he said. 'I beat myself up all the time about it, more than anyone can. Anyone can talk about me all they want, I don't care. If, looking back on it, if I didn't do these things and didn't do that, maybe, maybe, what if? That's never gonna leave me ever, ever.'

* * *

In an hour-long interview, Jason had answered many of the questions Sue had been stewing over for four years.

Yes, he had injected her with ice. No, he didn't think he'd ever seen her inject herself. No, he couldn't recall if he had injected her on the day she died. No, he hadn't been drug-tested. Yes, he'd told police he and Lyla were on ice.

Sue had wondered how it was possible that Jason, an ice user, had slept for nearly twelve straight hours.

He said it was because drug use had kept him and Lyla awake for seven straight days, and he was crashing. 'When you've been up for seven days with no sleep, you just hit the pillow and you're gone. You're just out,' he'd told Kathryn.

Of course, Jason's story didn't answer all of Sue's questions – and it raised some new ones too.

There were several parts she just couldn't accept.

She found it strange he couldn't remember if he had injected Lyla that night, and wondered what else he couldn't remember.

She questioned whether he would truly have responded to Lyla's aggression by calmly telling her he was going to bed.

She wondered whether Lyla had tried to open the car doors when he did go to bed, and whether Jason had in fact locked her out of the car.

She questioned why, when he got up in the early hours of the morning and saw Lyla's bag on the ground, he concluded she had likely gone to her friend's house. Why would she –

at a time when she was angry with Jason – have left the car without her handbag?

For Sue, Jason's interview also cast even more doubt over the extent of the police investigation into Lyla's death.

How could an impromptu media interview with Jason, conducted outside a suburban shopping centre, have revealed more in one hour than the report of a detective who had worked on the case for more than a year?

Sue didn't have the answers to those questions. Once again, she was left feeling like her daughter's case just had not been a priority.

'It's just like no one gives no regard for Aboriginal people,' she said.

* * *

Lyla's brother felt similarly. When they spoke, Thibul Nettle told Kathryn he had thought a lot about the way his sister's death was handled by police.

'It makes you feel sad, because it just makes you think they're not important enough, Aboriginal women aren't important to investigate thoroughly,' he said. To think of a woman just lying there, like Lyla had been, was the worst thing ever, Thibul said.

He was warm and open and easy to talk to, like his mum, and like he told us Lyla had been. He often smiled as he spoke about his sister, but there was sorrow in his voice as he explained how his life had been completely upended by her sudden loss. They'd been close their whole lives – even through the ups and downs of Lyla's drug abuse – and had been through a lot together.

Thibul said he never judged Lyla, and she never judged him. That was the beautiful thing about their relationship. Their love for each other was truly unconditional.

'When I had issues, Lyla was the person I used to go to. Even if I needed a place to live, I'd just move in with Lyla.'

Being with his sister was 'just peace', he said. 'Similar to Mum.'

Years later, he was still struggling with her loss. 'She's gone, Mum's in Bali – I don't really have an outlet person to go to,' he said.

It hurt for Thibul to think about Lyla lying dead on the side of Port Wakefield Road as if no one cared about her. Because the truth was that so many people did.

'I know people do care, because Aboriginal culture, that's our main thing. Caring. Family,' he said. 'So she would have had a lot of family looking for her and caring where she was and stuff like that.'

When Kathryn asked what he thought had happened to Lyla, Thibul said he didn't know, and that all he had to go on was what the police had said. He felt it was only when investigators were put under pressure and pushed to go deeper that you could ever really know.

As an Aboriginal person, it wasn't difficult for him to believe that police might investigate some deaths more thoroughly than others. For Thibul, like Douglas, that indifference had been a fact of life while he was growing up and finding his place in the world. As Douglas had observed, deaths in their community were 'just written off'.

But it shouldn't be that way, Thibul said.

'I feel like it's neglect. I always say to Mum, if you're a police officer and you're not doing your job properly, then don't be a police officer. Because it affects people's lives.'

* * *

A few weeks after we interviewed Jason, hundreds of thousands of people read and listened to Lyla's story when it was published by the *Advertiser*. The story didn't tell the audience what to think, but instead presented them with the facts and let them decide.

The response was overwhelming. Like Sue, many were astounded that she had not received answers, given the circumstances of her daughter's death. For Sue, it felt like validation – and like hope that someone might finally listen to her concerns.

Police declined to comment on the story before publication, but Sue hoped someone at SA Police had seen or heard it. The issues she had spent years trying to raise had finally been laid out for the world to see, and she thought it might prompt the police to contact her.

But, again, she heard nothing. There was no follow-up about the new information, no talk of re-questioning anyone or re-examining any aspect of the case, and they offered no explanation or apology for the gaps in the official investigation.

Frustrated but by no means shocked, Sue wrote to the detective. In October 2023, on the day that Lyla would have turned forty-four, she sent a long email outlining all of her outstanding questions and concerns.

She set out, one by one, what she saw as the inconsistencies in Jason's story, and revisited many of the issues she had raised previously that she felt police had never addressed, including the fact that Jason had admitted to injecting Lyla with ice earlier that week, and also the fact that Lyla had been messaging a friend in the early hours of 17 May about her plans for that day.

'When do police take seriously what families say about their child, the information provided, the questions asked?' Sue wrote. 'I'm still suffering, still searching for answers, still hoping there will be justice.'

Again, it took more than two months to receive a short

Lyla Nettle

reply, which came – only after Sue had followed up, asking for a response – on 27 December.

It read:

Good afternoon Susan,

I hope that you are well.

I am sorry for yours and your family's loss of Lyla and can only imagine that it will be particularly felt at this time of year.

Thank you for the additional information that you provided. I have passed it on to the Coronial Investigation Section for further consideration.

If you come in receipt of any further information that you feel is important, please feel free to email me.

Sue felt sure it would lead to nothing, but she could at least take comfort in knowing that she had done everything in her power to draw her concerns to the attention of police.

Then, something unexpected happened. On 4 January 2024, another email came. This one was sent by a different detective.

I am making some follow-up enquiries on behalf of Special Counsel, State Coroner's Court, relative to the death of your daughter, Lyla. I have been advised that Lyla had a best friend she was conversing with in the early morning of 17 May 2019. Are you able to provide me her full details and any contact details you have for her?

Lyla's friend later confirmed she had spoken to the police, but, as Sue had feared, nothing seemed to come of it.

On 28 February 2024, the *Advertiser* sent a series of detailed questions to the police:

1. Lyla's mum, Susan Nowland, was contacted earlier this year [SA Police, advising that police were] 'making some follow-up enquiries on behalf of Special Counsel, State Coroner's Court, relative to the death of your daughter, Lyla'.
   — What prompted SA Police to continue investigating the death of Lyla Nettle? Did the coroner's court request that SA Police continue investigating?
   — Is SA Police currently investigating the death of Lyla Nettle?
2. Lyla's partner, Jason, told the *Advertiser* that he introduced Lyla to injecting methamphetamine, he never saw her inject herself and he injected her on the week she died. He claims to have also told police this when he was interviewed after Lyla's death.
   — Given these admissions, why hasn't Jason been charged with administering a drug of dependence?

198

3. Following the publication of the *Advertiser*'s stories
   last year, Ms Nowland wrote a lengthy email [to
   SA Police] to highlight new evidence in the case. The
   email was sent on 20 October but she received no
   response until 27 December.
   — Why has it consistently taken SA Police months
     to acknowledge emails from Ms Nowland? Does
     SA Police consider this to be an acceptable way to
     treat relatives trying to raise issues?

SA Police declined to answer specific questions, replying with
this statement:

SAPOL takes very seriously the investigation of any
sudden death. These matters were investigated, which
found no suspicious circumstances. The matters are now
with the coroner and any further questions should be
directed to the coroner's office.

* * *

A full moon is sacred in Bali. Each month, the island's large
Hindu population gathers at local temples to mark the occasion
with a special ceremony called Purnama. They prepare offerings
of gratitude and worship Sang Hyang Chandra, a lunar deity,
as a way of cleansing the body and soul.

DYING ROSE

Sue has her own full moon ritual. As the moon rises over Candidasa, its reflection glistening over the Bali Sea, she climbs three storeys of stairs to the top of one of the main buildings of the resort where she lives. The roof is a large open space with ochre tiles, a gazebo and a few scattered seats. Up there, she lights a stick of incense and, through her phone speakers, she plays Kane Brown's song 'Heaven'. The love-drunk hit had been Lyla's favourite just before she died.

Then, with only the full moon for company, Sue dances.

She finds comfort in this ritual, in its consistency. After this full moon, there will be another, then another, then another. A constant in a life of unknowns.

As certain as the lunar calendar, Lyla's memory will live on.

SHANARRA BRIGHT CAMPBELL

The footage is harrowing.

Police jostle around a bathroom door. The bathroom is tucked under a steep staircase in a small, crowded flat.

A woman is filming the police. She is in the living room, just metres from them. You can hear her swearing at them, screaming, 'Don't hurt my son!' and 'Oh my god!' Her view of what is happening is partly obscured by a cot.

Somewhere behind her, you can hear medical machines beeping.

'My daughter's *dead*,' she cries. She gives a gut-wrenching sob, her breathing loud and rapid.

As she turns, the camera pans briefly past two St John Ambulance paramedics, backlit by bright morning sunlight, performing CPR on a young woman lying on a mattress.

The police pull a young man from the bathroom and push him to the floor. Four of them take a limb each and start dragging him towards the open front door of the flat. 'You're breaking my fucking arm!' the young man shouts.

The paramedics look up as the police push past them. There is no room. They have to lean in over the young woman's body to continue chest compressions as the police drag the young man out the door.

* * *

Douglas Smith found the video in his inbox in February 2023. It was accompanied by an email.

> Hi Douglas,
> This is footage of a working family in Alice Springs, Northern Territory.
> The mother woke with the suicide of her daughter, rang ambulance, but taskforce police were deployed.
> The police force their way into the property, pepper-spraying the sibling. Sibling went to wash his eyes from the pepper spray. Police officers went into the bathroom, tasered and brutally bashed and attacked the mother's son.
> Northern Territory police force covered all up, the Northern Territory government cover it up.
> With no justice within Australia or Northern Territory ... No one in Australia wants to take this case on.
> Kind regards
> Lena-Rose Campbell

Shanarra Bright Campbell

* * *

The video had been taken in Lena-Rose Campbell's lounge room at the Keith Lawrie Flats in Alice Springs on the morning of 4 October 2019. Lena-Rose had filmed it herself, on her phone.

Her daughter Shanarra had chosen that morning to end her own life.

Just after 7 am, Lena-Rose had woken with a chilling feeling that she just couldn't shake. She knew instinctively something was wrong.

'It's like something was telling me to get out of bed and wake up,' she would tell Douglas when they met. 'It's hard to explain, really. It was almost as if my daughter was saying something to me.'

Upstairs, her eldest, Justin, was fast asleep. In the living room on a mattress, sleeping next to Lena-Rose, were her three youngest children. They usually slept in the living room together.

Then she heard her niece screaming at the back door. Lena-Rose leapt up and ran to her. She looked out at the yard and started screaming too.

Shanarra had hanged herself from the clothesline.

Lena-Rose's legs gave way and she collapsed, shouting for Justin.

Her son had quickly run downstairs and outside. He laid Shanarra on the ground, then he and Lena-Rose carried her into the living room and put her on the mattress, where they tried to resuscitate her.

Lena-Rose had already called triple zero and was expecting an ambulance to arrive. Instead, it was the police who came.

'They were there in seconds. My son was quite distressed. He didn't want the police coming in. He just wanted the ambulance,' Lena-Rose said.

But the police just kept coming. Soon there were three police cars out the front of the house.

The NT Police haven't said anything publicly about what happened next. What appears irrefutable is that Justin was pepper-sprayed; he then rushed to the bathroom, followed by police, to wash his eyes in the shower.

It was then that the paramedics arrived.

When Justin turned around, the police were there behind him.

'And then that's when they started this bashing,' Lena-Rose said. 'Bashing him up when he was in the shower.'

Already in shock, she started screaming at them not to hurt him. That's when she took out her phone and started filming.

It might already have been too late to save Shanarra – but that wasn't yet clear.

Either way, while her life was coming to its grim end, the police were fixated on Lena-Rose's son, not her daughter.

'They weren't there for her,' Lena-Rose said. 'They were more or less worried about bashing my son.'

* * *

When Lena-Rose describes her eldest daughter, the word that comes to her most freely is 'bubbly'. Shanarra Bright Campbell had burst into the world at the Women's and Children's Hospital in Adelaide in July 1996, a bubbly, bouncy newborn. Her best friend was already waiting to meet her when she made her grand entrance: her older brother, Justin Goldsmith. He was two years old at the time and completely besotted by the new addition to his family. Their mother was tired but happy, having just given birth to her second child.

It was not long after Shanarra was born that Lena-Rose realised she had to acknowledge a few facts. She was single, and both Shanarra and Justin had different fathers, neither of whom was in the picture, so it would just be the three of them. Life was going to be a bit tougher for Lena-Rose than it is for some, and she'd have to find a way to make it work. She wanted a stable home for Justin and Shanarra, somewhere their little family could be comfortable.

Lena-Rose wasn't sure what she was going to do, but she knew Adelaide, a mid-sized city, wasn't where she wanted to raise her children. She thought about moving the three of them to Darwin for a 'better life', as she put it, and spent the next six months saving up every dollar she could. She would eventually make it halfway, setting up house in Alice Springs, in Australia's Red Centre. It was in the Northern Territory, like Darwin, but about as far away from the tropical northern capital in terms of climate and culture as you could get.

It was far from Lena-Rose's country, too: her people were Ngarrindjeri, from Raukkan, about eighty kilometres south-east of Adelaide, and Narungga, from the Yorke Peninsula. That didn't worry Lena-Rose, though. 'We just had to get out of South Australia,' she said.

On her father's side of the family, Shanarra belonged to the Adnyamathanha, the original custodians of a vast swathe of the majestic Flinders Ranges in South Australia's Mid North. Shanarra would never really connect with her father, although she did spend time with his family, and she took his name, Bright. It was fitting for a girl who was so bright by nature.

Lena-Rose says she was always a fast learner, right from the start, picking up how to walk at just nine months of age – three months earlier than average. From then on, Shanarra and Justin had been inseparable, exploring their new home in Alice Springs together.

In time, Shanarra and Justin would become older sister and brother to two more sisters and a baby brother, Reeshay, Jacinta and Jerome, as Lena-Rose's little family grew. The role of older sister was one Shanarra treasured. She had strong mothering instincts and showered her younger siblings with love and care. Even Justin, two years older than Shanarra, was part of her brood.

'She would always make sure we were all okay before herself,' Justin said. 'And she was always angry at us if we did the wrong thing. She was like a second mother to us.'

Shanarra loved to do fun things with her brothers and sisters, and when she found a place worth visiting, she made sure they were right next to her. Her outgoing spirit took the siblings on many adventures.

'Sometimes she'd get itchy feet,' Justin said. 'She'd just get up and be like, "C'mon, we gotta go, this is what we gotta bring and we're going over here."'

Shanarra and Justin remained close as they grew older, right through school and on into high school. He said she was always joking, always had a smile on her face. The two of them, brother and sister, were the glue that bonded their group of friends together.

Shanarra had a purity to her. Pure kindness, pure love and pure joy. She loved to cook for people, to look after them, to make them happy. She grew up to work with kids with disabilities and cared for her own loved ones too.

But inside, Justin said, his sister sometimes felt empty. She spent so much time caring about and helping others that she forgot about herself.

* * *

It is hard to reconcile the picture of the smiling, joking Shanarra, full of pure joy, with the fact that she chose to take her life when she was just twenty-three. Sadly, though, almost a quarter of the deaths of Aboriginal girls and women in their teens and early twenties are caused by intentional self-harm. First Nations people are nearly three times more likely to die by suicide than other Australians, as noted in our discussion of Rose Hunter-Hebberman's death. But that shocking figure is in large part due to the high proportion of suicide deaths among *young* First Nations people.

It was a story about young people in Alice Springs, the town where Shanarra grew up, that first brought Douglas there, to the heart of Australia, in February 2023.

Alice Springs, or Mparntwe as it is called by the Arrernte people, its traditional owners, was built on the Todd River, which, unless there is a cyclone up north, is not so much a river as a stream, or a dry, dusty bed. Once a thriving outback hub, the town had recently become the centre of national attention when the mayor called for the army to be brought in to restore order to its streets. Australians were tuning into the nightly news for a running commentary on the crisis, brought on by the antisocial behaviour of 'wayward' Aboriginal youth.

Gemma had asked Douglas to visit Aboriginal communities in the Red Centre to find out why so many young people were out of control. She wanted him to try to get right to the heart of what was happening there.

The stories Douglas filed from Alice Springs painted a heartbreaking picture of extreme disadvantage, making the national story of violent Aboriginal kids wreaking havoc on the streets a far more complicated one. The headline on one story said it all. '"We are the lost tribe of Alice Springs": The families living in third-world conditions just five-minute drive from town centre'.

Douglas was reporting from Irrkerlantye, also known as White Gate, one of the seventeen 'town camps' surrounding Alice Springs, where the twenty residents were living in tin sheds. These tin structures – barely even humpies – dotted the camp. The people living in them fried in summer and froze in winter, sleeping on filthy mattresses atop log stump bases with equally filthy bedding on top. There was no electricity, no running water. The squalor could not be overstated.

A local Elder said she had been agitating for forty years for conditions in Irrkerlantye to improve, but nothing had ever been done. She told Douglas how hard it was to get kids cleaned up for school when there was no running water and no way to heat what water you do have in winter.

This was all just a five-minute drive from the heart of Alice Springs.

Douglas's story was widely read online and made the front page of the *Advertiser*. Only a month later, having waited forty years, the community had clean drinking water – not due to government action, but because Douglas's reporting reached a relative of his living in the United States, Olympic medallist and US National Basketball Association hero Patty Mills. Without prompting from Douglas, Mills had paid for the installation of a water treatment plant for the community.

Douglas's trip to Alice Springs had helped to illuminate the overwhelming poverty that was the backdrop to the town's youth crime crisis, sparking action that benefited at least one community.

It would also be the catalyst for Shanarra's family to get in touch with him.

* * *

The week after Douglas came back from Alice Springs, he opened his computer to find an email with the subject line: *Two weeks before Kumanjayi Walker was shot evidence.*

Like most Australians, Douglas was across the Walker case and so the mention of it in the subject line of the email caught his attention.

Walker, a nineteen-year-old Warlpiri-Luritja man, had been shot dead by a Northern Territory Police officer, Zachary Rolfe, on 9 November 2019. It had happened in Yuendumu, a remote community three hundred kilometres north-west of Alice Springs.

Walker had stabbed the officer in the shoulder with scissors while resisting arrest. Rolfe responded by shooting him three times at close range. The shots were fired at 7.22 pm; Walker died at the police station in Yuendumu at 8.36 pm. His family were not notified of his death until 8 am the next morning.

The case became a flashpoint for racial tension around the country.

Rolfe was charged with murder, which in the Northern Territory attracts a mandatory life sentence with a minimum non-parole period of twenty years.

The white police officer argued that he had shot Walker in self-defence. In March 2022, after a five-week trial, a jury in the Supreme Court of the Northern Territory deliberated for seven hours before acquitting him of the murder charge and two alternative charges, manslaughter and engaging in a violent act causing death.

A coronial inquiry began in Alice Springs on 5 September 2022. When Rolfe appeared before the coroner in February 2024, the insights his testimony gave into the attitudes of police to Aboriginal Australians at the time of Walker's death were deeply disturbing.

Rolfe admitted to using racist language before he dropped bombshell allegations: that the Northern Territory Police's elite response group unit held an awards ceremony for 'c—n of the year', at which the officer who had 'exhibited the most c—n-like behaviour' was recognised.

'The staff would make the recipient dress up in a toga and they'd give him a wooden club with some nails through the end,' Rolfe told the court.

There were also claims in the coroner's court that police had referred to Aboriginal people as 'bush c—ns' and 'sand n—as', and that one had called a woman a 'fat g—', a highly offensive term for an Aboriginal woman.

A section of a local pub, the Todd Tavern, frequented by Aboriginal drinkers in Alice Springs, was called the 'animal bar' by police, Rolfe alleged.

Rolfe's own texts revealed his use of racist language, something he claimed to regret.

'The fact that I, for example, said c—n in my messages, the fact that that's been made public, which would have caused hurt to a number of people, especially kids, who should have been able to trust the police force, that kills me, so I am sorry for that, but I can't take it back,' Rolfe said.

Three senior police then swore affidavits to deny the 'c—n awards' existed, prompting Rolfe in response to produce a certificate, printed on an Aboriginal flag, awarded 'for lack of hygiene and incompetence'.

It appears the awards were renamed in 2022, but the evidence left the police brass reeling. Rolfe's testimony had illuminated the relationship between police and Aboriginal communities in Central Australia and in the Northern Territory more generally.

Shanarra Bright Campbell

* * *

It was Lena-Rose Campbell who had sent the email to Douglas. She thought one of the police officers who had responded to her triple zero call was Zachary Rolfe – just five weeks before he had shot Kumanjayi Walker.

The *Dying Rose* team began investigating Shanarra's case and found that although Lena-Rose was confused on that point – Rolfe had not been among the police who came to her house the day Shanarra died – there was a shocking story to tell about how the officers dealt with her daughter's death.

Unlike other, similar tragic deaths around the country, the way authorities had handled the final moments of Shanarra's life would come under the microscope – but not until she had already been gone for several years, when the problems in Alice Springs exploded onto the national stage.

As we would learn, the place where Shanarra ended her life had been no stranger to tragedy. The Keith Lawrie Flats in the suburb of Gillen, in the inner-west of Alice Springs, are a block of public housing units notorious in the town. Since the twenty-five basic, boxy two-storey homes made of cheap materials were constructed in the 1970s, the complex had been plagued by drug and alcohol abuse, violent assault and murder. Keith Lawrie Flats are a place where even hope goes to die.

The complaints from residents and neighbours are so constant that police and paramedics are daily visitors. In

215

recent years, residents in the local area have come together to raise their concerns about ongoing antisocial behaviour at the housing complex.

The member for the seat of Araluen in the Northern Territory parliament, Robyn Lambley, helped residents advocate for the sale of the flats to private buyers, or the total demolition of the block by the Department of Housing.

She held meetings where Aboriginal women who called the complex home spoke of 'living in fear' of the alcohol-fuelled violence and break-ins.

The Department of Housing had agreed to move at least one woman to help to address the debilitating stress induced by life at the complex.

In December 2017, Lambley wrote in the *Alice Springs News* that 'people have had enough'.

But controversy at Keith Lawrie Flats was nothing new. A decade before, the residents had all been shipped out so the block could undergo a facelift. Most of the original residents declined to move back, such were the problems they had experienced there.

'These people expressed how completely and utterly fed up they are with the daily screaming and yelling; the fighting; the daily visits by the police and ambulance to the flats; the daily 'drinking parties' in the complex; and the endless stream of visitors disrespecting the rights of residents,' Lambley wrote.

There was a stigma attached to the housing complex where Lena-Rose and her family had lived – but for them, it was a roof over their heads. At the time, Lena-Rose was a working single mother of five, and they had all lived together in the tiny two-bedroom flat. They were a close family, and Lena-Rose had thought of it as cosy. She loved her children fiercely and they loved her in return.

She worked in the aged care sector, looking after the elderly – she was a loving mum, just trying to provide the necessities of life for her brood. As a single mother, though, it is a reality of life in Australia that you can hold down a job and still be forced to bring up your children in, and surrounded by, poverty.

'We're working people – we're quiet, working people,' Lena-Rose told us when we began our investigation. 'I was working. I was ready to go to work that morning.' Her son Justin had also been working casually in construction at the time.

Shanarra had been working in mental health as a counsellor, but she had been unemployed and looking for work elsewhere at the time of her death.

* * *

Shanarra had died at home, and it was too painful for her family to stay there. After her death, Lena-Rose had moved

DYING ROSE

away to Darwin – as she had once dreamed of doing – with her remaining four children.

When Douglas flew to Darwin to visit her, it was in the new home she shares with her children, another small two-bedroom unit, in the suburb of Malak, surrounded by lush, tropical green grass. Their new life is a long way from Alice Springs and the red desert, but Shanarra is never far from their thoughts.

As you walk in through the front door, a series of photos hanging on the wall show Shanarra smiling with her mother and siblings. You can almost feel the trauma and pain the family has been through when you see how they're living: Lena-Rose has been unable to throw out Shanarra's clothes and other belongings, and they are all around, cluttering the kitchen table and other surfaces, filling the family's living space. It's as though Lena-Rose is holding on to Shanarra's possessions because she can't let go of what happened to her and her family on the day her daughter died.

Douglas sat opposite Lena-Rose and Justin in the modest living room and took out a tape recorder. He asked them to tell the story of what happened that day. He started by recording an interview ID: 'State your name, your mob, where you from?' he said.

Lena-Rose shared her account of that day with him, explaining what he and Gemma had seen in the video she had sent him.

Then it was Justin's turn.

'This is on record,' Douglas said. 'Speak up if you can, brother.'

As Justin began to speak, it was clear that he was reliving that day in his mind.

'We carried her inside and then laid her on the bed. We did CPR and tried to resuscitate her,' he said.

He remembered his mother calling an ambulance. He said he was in shock when police arrived, and that he hadn't wanted them to come in.

There was a commotion over his refusal to let the police in, and he had sworn at them, telling them his sister needed an ambulance, not police, telling them to wait outside, wait until the ambulance had come.

His mum was screaming, and he was crying. They blasted him in the face with pepper spray and forced their way into the house. His eyes and face burning, he ran for the bathroom. He remembered hearing one phrase amid the chaos that followed: 'resist arrest'.

'I was still washing my face, and then after that they came in and told me, you know, you're under arrest.' That was the moment that prompted Lena-Rose to turn her phone camera on.

'They were like, booting me and everything and stepping on my head. I just wanted to see my sister, you know? I wanted to see my sister.'

He was taken outside to a paddy wagon and forcefully manoeuvred inside in a way that 'knocked him around a bit'. Justin recalls arguing with police, who said he had hit them. He also says he remembers one officer telling him they 'had it all on camera'.

Justin was conveyed to the police station. He was then taken to hospital before he was eventually allowed to return home.

Following his arrest, Justin said, he was charged with assault, resisting arrest and hindering police. He and his mother were drowning in grief, and at the same time expecting he'd be called up to court at any moment to answer the charges against him.

Then the weirdest thing happened. Nothing happened at all. They didn't hear from police or from the court.

Justin decided to head into the local police station to find out when he was due in court.

The police checked their system and told him there were no charges.

'They said, "No, nothing's here." And I said, "You sure?" And they're like, "Yeah, no, no, nothing's here for you." I couldn't get over it.'

He was sure he'd been charged, but it seemed there was no record of it – and if there were no charges, why had he been arrested in the first place?

The family has since asked to view police body camera footage from that day, but they have never been shown any footage, or even told formally whether any exists. The Northern Territory coroner's office later declined Douglas's requests to release any body-worn camera footage, without confirming such footage actually exists.

Justin had been left deeply traumatised by the events of that morning: not only finding his sister dead, but the treatment he and his family had received after calling for help. 'I don't wish that on anybody's family anywhere in Australia or in the world to have that sort of thing happen to them,' he said.

Justin and Douglas briefly compared notes on their experiences with the police as young Aboriginal boys. Both had developed a fear of being stopped on the street for questioning, and of the focus turning to them in any interaction with police, despite knowing that they had done nothing wrong.

Douglas acknowledged the feeling could be irrational, 'but as an Aboriginal person, you don't feel the police are there to help'. That feeling may help explain why Justin's instinct was to turn police away at the door on the day Shanarra died.

Justin said he couldn't get over how his family had been treated that day. How could anyone respond like that to people in such intense emotional distress?

Lena-Rose was quick to identify a cause. If they had been a white family, she asked, would they have been treated like that? Because they were black, they just weren't listened to.

Douglas sent the Northern Territory Police a series of questions, hoping to hear the police officers' side of the story. The response was brief.

Northern Territory Police will not be commenting on the matter.

* * *

For the family, the four years since Shanarra died had not been kind. Lena-Rose still couldn't sleep. She had nightmares and had been in and out of hospitals seeking treatment for the horrific trauma of losing her beloved daughter. She had become a nervous wreck and had to give up work.

Finding 'justice' had become an obsession, and she pursued it through whatever avenues she could, trying to get answers from police about why they had responded as they did that day.

In August 2021, almost two years after Shanarra's death, she had appealed for help from the Northern Territory's ombudsman's office, but drew a blank.

The assistant ombudsman wrote back to her:

While I was saddened to hear about your experience with police, I have had to carefully consider the resources we will allocate to the high volume of complaints received at our office.

I have considered your request to have this matter investigated, however, as the investigative process is a complex one, we need to carefully consider conduct occurring twelve months ago. With the greatest of reluctance I have decided on this occasion I am unable to accept this complaint.

Dismayed to learn that resourcing was all that stood between her and an ombudsman's investigation, Lena-Rose began frantically contacting lawyers and anyone she could find working in Aboriginal legal services, imploring them to take up the case.

Eventually, Sydney lawyer George Newhouse agreed to represent the family in making a formal complaint to the police.

With their lawyers, Shanarra's family went into a conciliation meeting with police. The two sides sat down and tried to come to an agreement without going to court.

They did come to an agreement, but it included a confidentiality clause. For that reason, exactly what was said and agreed to cannot be reported. We can report, however, that Shanarra's family wasn't satisfied with the outcome. With all avenues exhausted and now legally gagged, Lena-Rose retreated to her grief in private.

Mr Newhouse would later give evidence at the Senate Inquiry into Missing and Murdered First Nations Women and Children, which held a hearing in Sydney in July 2023.

DYING ROSE

The *Dying Rose* reporting team was there.

In giving evidence, Mr Newhouse echoed what Lena-Rose had said about how hard it was for them, and other Aboriginal families, to be listened to.

'With no meaningful accountability internally or externally, marginalised people have no recourse and are disempowered,' Mr Newhouse said.

He also called for a banning of non-disparagement and confidentiality clauses attached to settlements with police – like the one Lena-Rose and her family had agreed to – unless the victims wanted to remain anonymous.

On 14 September 2023, we released the *Dying Rose* episode telling the story of Shanarra Bright Campbell's death and the horrific way her grieving family had been treated. It was a compelling story, and one worth telling – even without knowing exactly how it had ended.

Lena-Rose said it was the first time she felt her daughter's story had truly been heard.

CHARLI POWELL

'Please help me!'

It was 4 am when the man, whom we'll call Stephen, was jolted awake by a frantic knock at the door.

It was early on Monday 11 February 2019. He had gone to bed at about 10 pm the night before, planning to wake at 5.30 am to get ready for work.

Stephen, then forty-two years old, lived in the suburbs of Queanbeyan, a regional New South Wales town just a stone's throw from Canberra. It was a quiet, residential area – most of Queanbeyan is – and any disturbance at night was unusual.

Wearing only his underwear, Stephen got up and cautiously approached the front door. It was open – the summer night had been hot – but the screen door was locked. On the other side of the screen was a young man – somewhere between sixteen and nineteen, Stephen guessed – with a baby face and dark hair and eyes.

'I think she's killed herself,' the young man said.

Stephen was wary – 'You don't know what happens at that time of night,' he would later observe – but the young man seemed to him to be in shock and suffering genuine grief.

'He was just very upset and obviously needed help, so I wasn't going to second-guess that,' Stephen said.

He put on a dressing gown and ugg boots, went outside and followed his late-night visitor down the street in the dark. They walked quickly, the young man a little ahead, to Freebody Reserve, about fifty metres away.

The recreational reserve was the site of sports games during the day, and a popular spot for dog walkers. There were usually lots of kids running around too, and queues at the bustling canteen – but late at night it was deserted.

The young man led the way to a men's toilet block at the edge of the reserve. It was a dingy old freestanding brick block with a concrete floor. There, they met with a confronting sight: a girl was slouched in the doorway, vomit and blood around her.

'I saw the deceased there on the ground,' Stephen later told the New South Wales coroner's court. 'And it was reasonably dark, but I noticed that there was clothing around their neck and they weren't moving.'

The young man bent down in disbelief and cradled the girl, saying words to the effect of 'She can't be dead.'

Together, the two men dragged her out of the toilet block and onto a grassed area and started CPR.

'I've done first-aid training before, so one of the things was sort of, you know, clear away the danger and then do CPR and that sort of thing,' Stephen said. 'So that's what we did after that. One did mouth-to-mouth, while the other did chest compressions.'

The young man had called an ambulance, which arrived a short time later. Paramedics asked both men to stand aside while they took over resuscitation efforts.

They stepped back, and then, as they watched the paramedics try to save the girl's life, the young man told Stephen that her family was going to bash him and kill him.

* * *

That girl was Charli Powell, just seventeen years old when she died. Born in October 2001 to parents Sharon Moore and Douglass Powell, Charli was adored by her large family and close circle of friends, who say she was vivacious, passionate and full of life.

'She was my second-eldest, and the craziest,' Sharon told the *Dying Rose* team. 'You know, I wonder if she actually knew she was gonna pass away young, because she just lived every day to the fullest. As she walked in the room, I know it's cliché, but it used to light up, like she just had that personality. She was always giggling, and she just made you laugh. She had a real crazy laugh. She was a good girl.'

Charli had grown up in Queanbeyan, on the lands of the Ngambri and Ngunnawal peoples, but she was descended from their neighbours, the traditional owners of the plains of central New South Wales. The Powells, Charli's father's family, were Wiradjuri people, and she was proud of that heritage.

Charli had attended Queanbeyan South Public School and then Karabar High School before she left during Year 10. To her best friend and classmate, Kaitlin Sanderson, the word that best described Charli was 'fun'.

'She was just so loud, everyone was always just drawn to her,' Kaitlin said. 'She was always just the life of the party, always had music pumping. You would hear her coming from miles through the hallways at school because she'd have a speaker just blaring.'

She always had people around her, and she was always smiling and laughing.

Kaitlin said Charli was also very proud of her appearance and liked to look her best.

'If not, she wouldn't leave the house,' she said. 'She'd come to school some days in grey on grey, and I used to think, *If I wore that I'd look like I broke out of jail.* She used to rock anything.'

In October 2018, Charli had started working part-time at the KFC in nearby Fyshwick. But Sharon said her dream was to be a forensic scientist. She wanted to help solve crimes, and to protect people.

'Growing up through school, she'd been bullied. And so she used to take people who were being bullied under her wing and look after them so, you know, they didn't have to go through what she went through, I guess,' Sharon said. 'She was a real good girl.'

In her short life, Charli had her share of challenges. She'd grown up around domestic violence, and by the time she was thirteen, there had been thirteen child-at-risk reports made about her. She had also come to police attention on about fourteen occasions by the time she was seventeen.

She had been in an ongoing conflict with another student at her school, and she'd been accused of assault. Another set of charges related to an assault against police.

Charli had been exposed to drug use; she was reported to have used cannabis regularly and might have used ice on occasion.

A coronial investigation into Charli's death, launched four years after her body was found, also uncovered allegations of violence by her boyfriend, though he denied it.

Charli had met her boyfriend, whom we'll call Logan, when she was fifteen. When they first got together, in April 2017, she'd been happy.

'It was her first serious boyfriend,' Sharon said. 'At the start everything was great – in the honeymoon period, as they say.' But before long Sharon began to notice a change in her bright, bubbly daughter.

'She fell in love hard, because it was her first boyfriend,' she said. 'But then, I don't know … he was always calling, like obsessive calling, all the time, constant. I just saw a decline in her mental health. She wasn't as happy, and she'd come home a bit sad.'

Kaitlin had noticed it too. About six months into the relationship, she said, things started going downhill. 'The violence started,' she said.

'We were at our old mate's house,' Kaitlin said, 'and he came there, didn't like that she was there. It was about two o'clock in the morning, I think – the cops got called, cause he was actually going off his head, smashing everything in the house, and she was trying to calm him down. From there on, it just got worse and worse.'

Sharon had been in violent relationships in the past too. The coroner's report into Charli's death noted that Sharon had experienced domestic violence.

'There's nothing worse than watching your own child go through it,' Sharon said. 'I started telling her some stuff that I hadn't told anybody about my situation, and she opened up and she started telling me some stuff.'

Kaitlin recalled a concerning incident in November 2018, just a few months before Charli died.

'He followed her to school,' she said. 'I remember she jumped the back fence down the bottom corner, and she was covered in blood, her trackies were ripped. We kind of picked up that he'd got into her. She had scratches on her face, her whole face was bleeding. I remember I went up to the bathrooms with her and tried to wash it off … because she didn't want anyone to see that.'

Records show Logan was charged with assault but not convicted – the charges were dropped after Charli died, and he later denied it happened.

Kaitlin said that, after it happened, Logan said he knew what he had done was wrong.

'Two hours later, she was on my phone, because she didn't have a phone, and he was apologising to her, saying that he would never hit her again and that he was so sorry,' she said. 'It was a cycle from there on in.'

In December 2018, Sharon contacted Youth Justice NSW and told them Logan had assaulted Charli again.

It's unclear what the agency did about that.

The coroner noted that, in January 2019, it was alleged that Logan had fractured one of Charli's ribs by pushing her when they were on a camping trip. When Charli died the following month, an autopsy noted she had a healing fracture to her rib. Logan denied this was caused by him.

Sharon was shocked by the details of what her daughter had endured.

'What blows my mind is, they were both the same age.' Logan had also been around fifteen when he and Charli first started going out. 'What's a fifteen-year-old boy doing, at that age ... ? I can't get my head around it,' Sharon said. And it had only grown worse over time. 'It was getting to the point where it was every day, like every day.'

Charli would sometimes live with Sharon, and other times with Logan.

'I started to notice she was actually cutting herself, and started self-harming,' Sharon said.

Logan would eventually tell the inquest into Charli's death that their relationship was 'fucking toxic'.

'It wasn't a very good relationship. We were both young and ... we didn't know what the fuck to do. I understand that there were mistakes there, you know,' he said.

In her statement, Logan's own mother said she told Charli 'lots of times' that she should break it off with Logan.

The coroner called the relationship 'abusive'.

Logan had Charli's number saved in his phone under the name 'slut', which he said he had probably done after an argument. He said their relationship was 'pretty up and down' and they were 'always fuckin' arguing and shit'. They fought about both of them cheating, and Logan admitted he used to threaten Charli.

Among the jealous, controlling and abusive messages he sent, one read: *I swear to God you slut around on me, I'll stab ya in ya throat.*

Kaitlin knew that he'd used that word about Charli.

'Every time she threatened to break up with him, it was always, "You wait, slut,"' she said. 'One time I remember she said she was going to break up with him and he threatened to come stab her.'

Logan told the inquest he had not been violent towards Charli at any stage, including in the period just prior to her death.

But the coroner disagreed.

'I do not accept his evidence in this regard,' she wrote in her findings, released in October 2022:

> The clear weight of the evidence supports a finding that [Logan] did make threats of violence and used actual physical violence towards Charli during their relationship. In my view that violence would have been a stressor for her and is likely to have contributed to her state of mind around the time of her death.

The coroner also made observations about the way Logan gave evidence during the inquest:

> He demonstrated an explosive temper when stressed. Even in the controlled atmosphere of giving evidence by AVL link from a correctional centre he was unable to manage his angry outbursts. Given the contemporaneous reports Charli made to her friends and family I have no

trouble accepting that Charli was subjected to [Logan's] rage on numerous occasions.

In about October 2018, Charli fell pregnant. But, adding to the distress of her relationship with Logan, she lost the baby.

Sharon was fed up. Her daughter was hurting, and it needed to stop.

'I saw a bruise on her cheek one day. I said, "That's it, Charli. I'm going up there. I've had enough, no more,"' Sharon said. 'And she got down on her hands and knees and she begged me, she said, "Please, don't go up there. Please, let me handle it." She only had a little frame, you know. She knew that he was stronger than her. And she tried to run, you know, but he'd always catch her. That's what she'd say, "He always catches me, Mum."'

The coroner accepted that Charli had no formal diagnosis of mental illness, and Youth Justice NSW had not recorded any concerns about her mental health or any risk of suicide. There was, however, evidence that Charli had untreated mental health issues in the lead-up to her death. Both Logan and Kaitlin said they were aware that Charli self-harmed, and Logan's mother said Charli had told her she'd first attempted self-harm when she was nine and had begun to hear voices in 2018.

The coroner approached the evidence of Logan and his mother on this issue with some caution. 'Nevertheless, I am persuaded that Charli is likely to have suffered significant stress which caused at least a serious mood disturbance from time to time,' she wrote. An autopsy conducted after Charli's death also found evidence of self-harm.

In early 2019, Kaitlin said that Charli decided she was going to end the relationship with Logan for good. After almost two years, she'd had enough, and this time she really meant it.

'It was the day after Australia Day, and we were sitting in Sharon's room,' Kaitlin said. 'I went up there to stay with her. She wrote a massive message. She was like, "I really do love you and I never wanted to give up on you, but I have to give up – I can't keep doing this."'

That decision seemed to have an immediate positive effect on Charli.

'The last two weeks, she was really happy,' Kaitlin said. 'I think I stayed there probably four times in those two weeks, and she was herself – she was really bubbly, she was really good.'

Sharon said that Charli didn't see much of Logan during that time. 'That was not like her at all,' she said.

But if Charli had been trying to end it for good, she didn't find it easy. The relationship seemed to start back up, and she began visiting Logan at his mother's place again.

On the Friday before her death, Charli worked a shift at KFC. Over the course of two-and-a-half hours that evening, Logan made seventy-seven unanswered calls to Charli.

The following morning, Charli sent a message to Logan at about 7 am that read: *I promise you, it's over forever.*

She later sent another message saying, *You treat me like shit, swear at me, abuse me, physically kick me out of your house at this time in the morning while I have a jumper and pyjama pants while I've been on my period.*

She blamed him for pregnancies she'd lost and said he had ruined her chances at a family and true love in the future. *I don't want any of it, all because of you,* she told him.

Between about 7.15 and 8.10 that morning, Logan made another ninety-seven unanswered calls to Charli. She asked him to stop calling.

He also sent her a series of messages via Facebook, in which he called her a slut, told her she didn't deserve a pregnancy and said, *Fuck you and your dead baby.*

Charli called him a 'junkie' and a 'woman basher'.

Logan also made repeated nuisance calls to Charli on the Saturday before her death, which the coroner found would likely have been 'intrusive and intimidating' for her.

In the last text message Charli sent to Logan, she threatened to leave him and tell every girl he was with that he was 'a woman basher and a liar and a cheater and most of all a user'.

According to Logan, they always made up after their arguments.

'That's how we – that's how we'd attack each other,' he told the inquest. 'We'd fuck, we'd fuck with our – each other's hearts, mate. I was seventeen. I was young. I didn't know how to respond to that shit. It was the first proper heavy relationship I had. She'd cut me deep, so I'd think, *How the fuck can I get her back?* and that's how I'd get her back.'

This occasion, he said, was no different, and by Sunday they had patched things up and were 'back to normal'.

On 10 February 2019, the day before she was found dead, Charli had gone to stay with Logan at his mother's house, not far from her own family home in Queanbeyan.

Sharon said she hadn't wanted her to go, but Charli was insistent. 'I said to her, "Stay, stay with me this weekend," and she was like, "I'll see how it goes up here, Mum."'

But it hadn't gone well. At one point, Charli called Sharon, upset.

'They were fighting, and she asked me to go pick her up,' Sharon said. 'My car was unregistered at the time, so I borrowed my mum's car and I rang her back, and I'm like, "I'll come up, I'll be there in like two heartbeats, I'll be there straightaway." But she said, "No, it's okay, Mum. Everything's okay now." She didn't sound okay.'

That was the last phone call Sharon ever had from her daughter.

* * *

DYING ROSE

In the years that followed Charli's death, Sharon was able to discover little about what had happened in the final hours of her daughter's life. First the distraught mother had relied on the police to find out. Then, when police said her daughter had died by suicide – which Sharon found hard to believe – she had looked to the New South Wales coroner for answers. For years, she had fought for a coronial inquest, and finally she had been successful. Now the inquest had come and gone, without giving Sharon the closure she had been yearning for. She still had so many questions, still felt that no one was listening to her.

It was in late 2022 that she contacted Courtney Hunter-Hebberman, whose daughter Rose's death was being investigated by the *Dying Rose* team. Just like Courtney, Sharon refused to let her daughter's story go untold – or to see what she believed was an inadequate response from authorities go unquestioned.

Courtney passed Sharon's number on to the *Dying Rose* team.

This mother, she wants to speak to you, Courtney wrote in a text to Kathryn. *Same case as Rose's almost.*

After a few messages back and forth, Kathryn and Sharon finally found the chance to speak on the phone. They spoke for more than forty minutes.

The story she told Kathryn was disturbingly familiar – and that is why, in May 2023, after several months spent researching stories very like Charli's, Kathryn caught a plane to Canberra.

* * *

Kathryn landed in the national capital on a brisk, blustery morning and headed straight for Queanbeyan, a commuter town on the New South Wales side of the ACT border, about fifteen minutes from the airport. Sharon had asked if they could meet at the home of Kaitlin, who had given birth to a baby boy with her partner, Charli's brother Lachie, just weeks earlier.

Every part the proud grandmother, Sharon introduced Kathryn to the bouncing bub the moment she arrived. Then, as Kaitlin settled the baby in his rocker, Sharon quickly made the reporter a steaming coffee and offered some Arnott's biscuits – a model of hospitality.

Kaitlin and Lachie's home was modest but tidy, and – Kathryn couldn't help noticing – packed with family photos, like Courtney's home in Adelaide, and Sue's villa in Bali.

While the welcome she'd received was warm, Kathryn could see that Sharon and Kaitlin were still grieving Charli. She knew the interview they were about to do would be painful for them.

More than four years on, they told her, they were still searching for answers about what had happened to Charli.

They had hoped the coronial inquest would clear things up, but it had left them feeling even less certain of the truth.

By the time the inquest was done, Logan had given three different accounts of the events leading up to the discovery of Charli's body in the men's toilet block at the oval: the first to police and ambulance officers at the scene on the day Charli died; the second, eight months after her death, in an 'ad hoc' police interview; and the third in evidence given at the coronial inquest.

In her findings, even the coroner noted it was 'difficult' to know exactly what had unfolded due to Logan's conflicting accounts.

Just after 8 pm on Sunday night, Logan's mother had left for work. He said he and Charli then spent the evening 'chilling', smoking marijuana and watching TV before Charli at some point left the house. The events of the subsequent few hours remain hazy.

After Charli's body was found, Logan told a paramedic at the scene that Charli 'couldn't stay at the house' – that's why she had left. But a police officer at the scene recalled Logan telling her that he and Charli had had an argument.

He gave a second version of events to the police eight months later. The third version, given at the inquest, was mostly consistent with this second version: on both occasions Logan said that there had been a disagreement between them at about 3 am, because Charli wanted him to take the cushions off the sofa to make a bed on the floor but, 'being stoned', he had just wanted to sleep.

Logan told the inquest that Charli told him, 'I don't want to sleep on that maggoty couch,' and started 'flipping'.

He left out one detail at the inquest, though: he'd told the police the argument had started because he had smoked the last cone.

Logan denied having kicked Charli out or forced her to leave at any stage, and said that when she told him she was leaving, he had unlocked the screen door and she'd gone.

Whatever the reason, Charli had left the house. In a text message sent by Logan after her death, he said she'd leapt up, saying: 'I'm going down Mum's.'

But she never arrived there.

It was about 6 am the next morning, Monday 11 February 2019, that police knocked on Sharon's door. They said Charli had taken her own life.

'I remember I got a phone call at 6.49 in the morning from Sharon,' Kaitlin said. 'I woke up and I saw her name. At first I was like, "Nah, I gotta go back to sleep," but then I was like, "No, I better answer it, because it's 6.49." I just remember Sharon crying, saying, "Charli's … Charli's gone. Charli's dead." I dropped the phone and I just started screaming. My brother came running and was like, "What's going on?", and I remember I just said, "Don't say it, don't say it."'

On the morning they knocked on her door, Sharon asked the police what had happened. All they seemed to know was what Logan had told them.

He had told police that, not long after Charli left the house, she had called him.

In that call, he said, she was 'going off' at him, so he hung up. She called again, crying, and 'told him she was going to kill herself'.

In his first recounting of the story to police, he told them that it sounded as though her voice was echoing, so he had asked her where she was. He said it sounded like she was in a toilet, and that he'd thought it was the toilet at her mum's place – which is where she'd said she was headed. However, in a later account of that evening, he said Charli had said she was at a toilet block at the Roos Club – the local nickname for the Queanbeyan Kangaroos Football Club, at Freebody Reserve.

In both of these accounts, Logan told Charli he was coming to get her, then heard a phone hit the ground. He said he yelled, 'Pick yourself up!' – meaning that Charli needed to pull herself together. He said he'd put his phone in his pocket – with Charli still on the other end of the line – then left home and started searching for her.

Logan didn't want to call the police. He knew he was wanted on a warrant. So he took a bike from bushes near his home and began riding.

Logan's car became a key point of questioning by Sharon's legal representative, Michael Bartlett, at the inquest.

In his first police interview, Logan had said he'd searched for Charli on foot – that he'd run on foot to a toilet block about a kilometre from his house. 'We thought, *That story on its face is pretty unlikely*,' Michael said, 'and it turned out it wasn't true. He changed the story to where he was on a push bike.' Logan later admitted the bike was stolen, which was why he initially told police he had run – an inconsistency that had been worrying Sharon, adding to her doubt and distress.

When questioned about his decision to take the bike rather than his car, Logan said, 'I've come out of the house, I was going to take my car at the time, but that was parked up behind my mum's under a carport, so I would have had to reverse it out and weave it around all this fucking shit [on my mother's lawn], so I wasn't doing that ...'

Later, he said, 'It would have taken me longer to get the car out than to just go.'

Logan said he then set off on a desperate search to find Charli. His accounts of his movements from that point also vary.

In his police interview and in evidence at the inquest, he said he went to the Roos Club, because that's where Charli had told him she was, couldn't find her there, and then went to the Roos Club oval.

In later evidence, he said that although he was aware of the toilet block at the oval near the Roos Club, where he eventually found Charli, his mind had gone blank, and he'd set out for the skate park on Henderson Road, near Queanbeyan Station, to check the toilets there instead. Then he remembered the toilet block at the oval. 'So I pumped it down there,' he said.

The coroner described Logan's evidence as 'certainly confused and at times inconsistent'. When describing the discrepancies, the coroner said she had observed Logan's 'significant agitation and the trouble he had giving calm and linear accounts of his actions'. She said he 'became exasperated when his past version was read back to him' and 'often spoke quickly without any real attempt to order his thoughts'.

Michael Bartlett submitted that Logan's entire account should be rejected – and the coroner admitted she had sympathy for that submission. She found aspects of Logan's account, in particular the reason he travelled to the toilets, to have 'troubling aspects'.

'For example,' she wrote:

[Logan's] recollection that he was first directed to the idea that Charli was in a toilet because the sound quality of the call suggested she may be in her mother's bathroom appears to me to be quite implausible. Having seen the toilet where she was found I would be surprised if anything about the acoustics of that place would alert [him] to the kind of location it was. On the other hand,

Charli Powell

I see no reason for [him] to concoct an account of a bicycle journey to the skate park if it had not occurred. I regard it as likely that [he] was affected by cannabis and extremely stressed when he set off on his bike, and that his capacity to form a rational plan is likely to have been significantly impaired at this time. In this context his route is not inherently implausible.

Call records show that Logan made a first call to Charli at 3.39 am, and then received two short calls from Charli. He told the inquest he did not remember making the first call but maintained he had hung up on her. Records show there were then four short calls from Logan, with a fifth call at 3.47 am lasting two-and-a-half minutes. He then made four further short calls, before making a seven-minute call to Charli at 3.51 am.

The coroner noted that Logan's account of events did not match those call records. Logan could not recall if he had continued riding while making these calls, and he was unable to explain why there were repeated calls, what was said, or why there were two long calls between him and Charli in the records rather than one.

However, the coroner also noted that those calls were made at a 'time of great stress'.

When Logan arrived at the oval, he found Charli hanging in the entrance to the male side of the toilet block. She

DYING ROSE

was suspended by a pair of thin blue women's jeggings. In evidence, Logan described Charli's legs as being 'curled up', with her knees bent and her feet behind her. He said he could not see her feet touching the ground.

He said that he had attempted to do CPR before running to a neighbour's home for help. After that, he said, he called triple zero.

By the time the police arrived, Charli's body was on the ground, no longer hanging. State Emergency Services crews had set up a large tent next to the toilet block, shielding Charli's body from view.

Beside the block, a bright red push bike had been dumped. On the ground was Charli's pink Kathmandu backpack, its side embroidered with flowers. Inside were a gold coin and some court papers.

When Sharon and Kaitlin asked later that morning how Logan had got her body down, the police couldn't explain.

Because they hadn't asked him.

'They didn't second-guess him at all. They just took everything that he said and just ran with it,' Sharon said.

Kaitlin agreed: 'They never questioned how he got her down … He said that it [the ligature fashioned from the jeggings] was tight and then all of a sudden it was loose.'

Another thing Sharon found hard to understand was the way the police had treated Logan that morning. At the time of Charli's death, there was a warrant out for his arrest: he

248

was facing charges for an assault on Charli, just across the border, in the ACT. One of the police officers who arrived at the toilet block that morning recognised him. She knew about the warrant, but not what it was for. Instead of arresting Logan, she told him, 'Go home, have a cup of tea, coffee, get physically sorted out and then come back to the police station.'

But he didn't come back.

When Sharon rang the police officer to ask why they hadn't arrested Logan, the officer said, 'I've actually listened to the triple zero call, Sharon – he sounds genuinely upset.'

Sharon said, 'How can you say that? How can you make that judgement? You don't know him!'

She said she got to the point where she was so frustrated that she went home to her mum and told her, 'It's like they're protecting him. I can't understand it.'

'I still can't get my head around it,' she told Kathryn.

The day after Charli's body was found, Sharon and Kaitlin went to see her at the funeral home. There, they found that she had a number of physical injuries.

'She had two big bruises on her cheeks, massive big bruises,' Sharon said. 'There was a big bruise in between her forehead that was actually raised.'

That bruise was noted in Charli's autopsy report. Sharon believed that it might have been inflicted by Logan, but he denied hitting her.

For Kaitlin, Charli's appearance also stood out. The vivacious, cheeky seventeen-year-old had always taken great pride in how she looked. But she'd been found in a pair of black and pink pyjama pants, a grey hoodie and a black and white t-shirt.

'She was in her pyjamas when she was found ... She never left the house in her pyjamas,' Kaitlin said. 'Even when people were coming over to her house, she would make sure that she was fully dressed and not in her pyjamas – makeup done, hair done. The fact that she was still in her pyjamas when she was found, that just doesn't make sense to me.'

Voice shaking, Sharon interjected, 'Police just believed it was suicide and that's what they ran with from the start.'

It was more than eight months after Charli died that the police caught up with Logan. He was arrested on other charges on 30 October 2019.

While Logan was in custody, the same police officer who had chosen not to arrest him on the morning of Charli's death finally interviewed him about what had happened that day.

According to the coroner, this interview occurred 'in an ad hoc manner, without preparation, when [Logan] had been using drugs and was facing considerable jail time for unrelated offences'.

'This meant that no immediate or detailed account was taken from the only person who had been with Charli in the period just prior to her death,' the coroner said.

Charli Powell

The coroner said she believed the decision not to interview Logan at the scene had 'unnecessarily increased suspicions in this case'.

'Even if a decision was taken to allow [Logan] to go home that evening, police should have monitored the situation or considered re-attending his home early the following day,' she said.

* * *

To see whether it was even possible for Charli to have suspended herself from the toilet block, Kathryn knew she needed to visit the site of Charli's final moments herself.

Sharon, Kaitlin and Kathryn piled into Kaitlin's Holden Astra hatchback. Kathryn sat in the back next to the baby, snoozing peacefully in his seat.

The two women showed her the meandering route, lined with red-brick houses, that they believed Charli would have taken from Logan's house to get to Freebody Reserve.

The toilet block was between the ground's two main ovals. As they approached it, Sharon became visibly upset. To this day, she doesn't understand why her daughter would have taken her final breaths outside the men's toilet, not the women's, which was just a few steps away.

'It still bothers me that it was the men's toilet, cause I know Charli and I know how much she hated the smell of them,'

Sharon said. 'It just doesn't make sense for her to go there – that's what's sticking out to me most of all. The men's toilet block just fucking bothers me.'

Police told Sharon they believed Charli went there because it was closer to the path she had taken.

'The officer goes, "No, we've already worked that out … It's because she would have walked this direction to get to the toilet block,"' Sharon said.

The toilets themselves were closed, with a locked gate barring the entrance. The brick exterior was painted an off-cream colour, with the chalk inscription *Love U CLP* on its walls. CLP was Charli: Charli Louise Powell.

Police said Charli, who was only 165 centimetres tall and weighed just fifty-two kilograms, had somehow shimmied her way up between two walls in a corner of the entryway until she reached a roof beam.

According to what Logan told police, she'd then managed to sling a pair of thin blue jeggings around that beam.

As far as Sharon knows, no tests were conducted until shortly before the coronial inquest, several years after her daughter's death, to assess whether those jeggings could or could not have borne Charli's weight.

'They didn't open those jeggings until court three years later … they'd never even pulled on them to see if Charli's weight could hold that,' Kaitlin said. 'I knew Charli's case had been neglected, but I didn't realise how badly until it all came out in court.'

One of the detectives who attended the scene later said the jeggings had creasing that was 'considered to be consistent with having been around Charli's neck', although he was unable to say how they had been secured.

There was also the question of how Charli had reached the beam. Standing where her body had been found and taking in the scene, Kathryn, who is 185 centimetres tall, realised that even she would struggle to make it up the wall.

It was not until well after Charli's death – again, just before the coronial inquest – that a reconstruction was performed to confirm that it was in fact physically possible for a person of Charli's height to reach the beam.

Somehow, though, Charli had also managed to tie the jeggings around the beam – according to Logan's evidence – while she was on the phone.

'She was on the phone to me when it happened – like, it all went quiet, but I dunno what happened,' Logan had told the coronial inquest.

The smell from the toilets was putrid. It was that stench that Sharon kept coming back to. 'Charli couldn't stand the smell of male toilets. She used to go off, saying, "Why do they stink so bad, Mum?" I just cannot see her walking to a men's toilet block to end her life when there's a female block directly beside it.'

DYING ROSE

Kaitlin shook her head. 'There were a couple of times Charli would say, "Should I ever do it [take my life], it'd be in bushland." When I found out it was at the toilets, it didn't make sense, especially because it was across the road from her little siblings' school. She would never have done that to them.

'I said to my mum, "That's not right. Charli didn't do that."'

* * *

Like many of the other mothers who spoke to the *Dying Rose* team, Sharon believed that the police response to her daughter's death was tainted by unconscious bias. She told Kathryn that Charli was known to police as a 'troublemaker' before she died. Sharon thought that history had affected the way the police looked at her death. That was why 'no one listened' when she asked how they could be sure her daughter had taken her own life.

'They were looking at me like I was just one of those mums trying to make trouble,' she said. 'But I know my daughter above anybody else. She was so strong-minded, and she always knew that tomorrow would be a better day, that it didn't matter what was going on. When the next day comes around, things are different. She knew that.'

When the police told her that Charli had died by suicide, Sharon knew that her only chance for answers would be a coronial inquest.

254

'They [the coroner's office] originally said no, so I got my solicitor to write back all the things that he thought were wrong with the case,' Sharon said.

For more than three years, Sharon pushed and pushed and pushed for Charli's case to be heard.

And on 1 March 2022, it was.

* * *

When the inquest started, Logan wasn't there in person. He was in prison, serving a ten-year sentence after pleading guilty to seventy-six charges resulting from a year-long crime spree. He had a number of criminal offences on his record that were made public during the course of the hearings, including burglary, aggravated burglary, arson, theft, assaulting a police officer and firearms offences; the majority of these offences had been committed after Charli's death, although, as noted previously, there had been a warrant out for Logan's arrest at the time that Charli's body was found.

But while Logan wasn't present, his family were there, and the tension between his people and Charli's hung in the air.

The coroner began by acknowledging the profound impact Charli's death had on her family

Over four hearing days, the court received extensive material including witness statements, police reports, medical records and court documents.

The inquest also heard oral evidence from officers involved in the investigation; from an expert forensic pathologist, Professor Johan Duflou; and from Logan, via video link from prison.

As noted earlier, even when giving evidence remotely, Logan was unable to control his anger, lashing out at those asking questions, but grief spilled over and rage flared on both sides. The proceedings were, at times, fiery. At one stage, tensions escalated so intensely that the coroner had to call for calm in the court.

'I don't want to kick anyone out of my courtroom – I never do – but I will if I have to,' she said on day four of proceedings. 'The last thing I want on the last day of this hearing, which has been so difficult, is to be involving sheriffs and police and having people ejected. I just don't want to see it. No matter how hard it is, we're all going to be respectful this morning.'

* * *

Michael Bartlett, who acted as Sharon's solicitor at the inquest, was a battle-hardened former police officer turned lawyer. Michael has decades of experience in both enforcing and prosecuting the law. He said his interest was piqued by Charli's case, particularly the decision to send Logan home 'for a cup of tea' after her body was found.

'I didn't think anyone was listening to Sharon's complaints … I still don't think anyone was listening,' Michael said.

When asked about NSW Police's response to Charli's death, Michael said that, in his opinion, the issues began early in the investigation.

'I was a policeman when I was young, so I've dealt with sudden deaths,' he said. 'You sort of have an idea what's meant to happen. To me, what happened with the police investigation was I think it went astray before they even got there. The ambulance officers rang it in to the police as a suicide, and the call went out to the car to attend. I think with the information they [the police] had been given before they got there, they [had] already decided it was a suicide. That meant they never even looked any further.'

In evidence given to the inquest, the police officer who recognised Logan said she had asked him briefly what happened before having a quick look around to 'check everything was safe, nobody else was injured'. She could not recall the content of her first discussion with Logan but had later taken a brief notebook statement. She admitted she knew that there was a warrant for his arrest but did not know what the warrant was for.

As the coroner's findings note, when pressed on why she did not arrest Logan, she stated, 'Because he was extremely upset, distressed, he just found his girlfriend. It wasn't the time to go and execute an outstanding warrant in my opinion.' During her evidence, the officer made it clear that she had considered herself to be investigating a 'suspected suicide'.

The coroner agreed with Michael's assessment that, while the decision made on 'compassionate impulse' to send Logan home was not legally problematic, it had potentially affected investigators' ability to establish exactly what happened that night.

She wrote:

> While I understand that she was concerned at [Logan's] level of distress when she decided not to take him into custody that night in relation to the outstanding warrant, I think it was somewhat naive to expect that [he] was going to have a cup of tea and then submit to arrest at the police station later that night or the following day ... [An] interview is only of interest to this court because of the effect that decision has had on the subsequent investigation into Charli's death. As it turned out [Logan] was not questioned for over eight months ... It is possible that an earlier interview ... may have produced a clearer account and decreased Charli's mother's suspicions in relation to the conduct of the investigation. It is also possible that an interview conducted in those stressful conditions would have added little to our understanding of the events just prior to Charli's death.

Even after the inquest, Michael said he was left baffled that an offender with a warrant out for his arrest was allowed to walk from the scene.

'[Logan has] got a warrant out, and the police constable said, "Oh, that's all right. I'm not going to arrest you, you can go." I can tell you now, I spent four years earning my living locking people up on warrants. In my experience, with that kind of warrant [that was issued against Logan], you never let them go. Ever.

'They knew he had a warrant, but they didn't actually get on the computer and do checks on him … all of that information was easily available. They didn't take a detailed statement from him at the scene. Police work is not that hard – but you've got to be a bit naturally suspicious.

'There are six questions you always have in your mind when you're looking at anything: what, when, where, who, why, how? That's it. You ask those six questions, and you start getting a picture of what happened. That didn't happen here.'

Michael said a formal interview with Logan immediately after Charli's body was found could have saved her family years of heartache and unanswered questions.

'It was crucial. It was crucial because, if you think about it, you've got a seventeen-year-old girl who's not hanging, and she's not been cut down,' he said. 'She had a dirty great big bruise in the middle of her forehead between her eyes – and they never asked how she got that.

'[Police have] got a dead girl. They've got a fellow there with a history of domestic violence who's wanted on a warrant – and he's giving them already, at that very early stage, highly inconsistent and conflicting stories.

'I was of the view that if police had been a bit more suspicious and diligent at the time, they would have been straight on to Logan, asking him serious questions about what's going on here.'

They didn't check Logan's car, he said. They didn't check the house. They didn't take a statement from the man whose door Logan had knocked on, asking for help. They didn't talk to his mother.

But what Michael found even more extraordinary was Logan's response whenever anyone tried to question him.

'He went right off his nut at them, screaming and yelling and swearing. In my twenty-five years of going to court, I've never had someone react like that. In my time in the police force, I have never, never had someone I've dealt with react that badly.

'I thought, *There are two things here. Someone who gives evidence in that fashion is, in my mind, not believable. They're not reliable.* The second thing I was thinking was, *I wouldn't want to be a seventeen-year-old girl in a house with this guy when he's behaving like this.*'

* * *

Another point of contention examined at the inquest was whether Logan had found Charli hanging – and, if he had, how he had managed to get her down.

Professor Johan Duflou had been the one to perform the autopsy on Charli's body. A highly experienced forensic pathologist, he has performed many thousands of autopsies over a forty-year career.

Professor Duflou told the court that while he could not 'absolutely exclude the possibility' of strangulation, in his opinion the evidence pointed to a death by hanging.

He said that the ligature mark, the lack of defensive wounds and the state of Charli's face were very much typical of hanging and would be 'very, very atypical for a case of ligature strangulation'.

The coroner put 'significant weight' on Professor Duflou's evidence.

She also took into account Charli's likely mental state before she died, and what she had experienced in the weeks leading up to her death.

In her findings, the coroner said she had no trouble accepting that Charli had been subjected to Logan's rage 'on numerous occasions'.

'Her death may well have been an impulsive act, but she had been subjected to significant verbal and physical abuse in the months before she took her own life,' she said. 'I have no doubt that impacted on the decision she made.'

She acknowledged that there were inconsistencies in Logan's evidence about how he found Charli hanging and that his account of events had changed between his initial police interview and examination at inquest.

'There is no doubt that the picture I have of the evening remains incomplete,' she said. 'I am somewhat uncertain about the nature of the disagreement Charli and Logan had prior to her leaving his home that evening. I will never know the exact content of the frequent calls between them that evening.

'I remain somewhat uncertain about the reasoning behind the course of Logan's journey around the suburb and exactly how he came to discover Charli in the male toilet block at Freebody Oval.'

Ultimately, though, she ruled that Charli's death was a suicide, shutting down speculation that Logan could have had a hand in her death. She said he did not appear to have been capable of such a sophisticated pretence:

I find it highly implausible that Logan strangled Charli and then successfully staged a crime scene that would suggest suicide, before deciding to act as the person who had discovered her body. There was nobody around. Surely if he had caused her death, the safest thing to do would be to leave her there for someone else to discover, especially when he was aware he had warrants for his arrest and knew he could be taken into custody if he had any contact with police.

These comments left Sharon distraught.

'I was very upset and angry about that. They don't know him on a personal level to say that,' she said. 'How can the coroner say he's not sophisticated? Does she know him? I don't know why they took his word as gospel. I really don't know, I really don't.'

* * *

The coroner set out her conclusions about the events of 11 February 2019 as follows:

It appears to me that following a dispute of some sort with [Logan], Charli left his home. It is possible that their dispute continued over the telephone. Terrible things were likely said. In these circumstances, in the middle of the night, alone and in a state of great despair, Charli made the decision to take her own life.

I am of the view that she communicated that intention to [Logan], who then attempted to find her. I am aware her family's shock indicates that they did not expect Charli to take such action and have taken into account the fact that Charli had recently got a job, that she was loved by friends and family, and that she had much to live for. However, tragically suicide is frequently shocking to those close to the deceased. It can be an impulsive decision, taken at a time of great distress.

I understand that Charli's family will be disappointed and possibly angered by this finding, and I am sorry to exacerbate the grief they are already suffering.

Before the coroner handed down her findings, Sharon had felt hopeful. She had entered the proceedings hoping that Charli's story would finally be heard and that police would be held to account for what she believed were the failings of the investigation, once the details were put before authorities. Instead, she left shattered.

'I fought so hard to get the inquest. But then they didn't do an investigation. They didn't even go and ask any of the neighbours in his street, nothing,' she said. 'They didn't ask them if they had seen or heard anything, didn't ask anyone at her work, didn't ring her work to check to see if she actually went to work. They didn't even go to his house.'

Michael Bartlett believed, like Sharon, that Charli's troubled background had influenced the way police approached her case.

'I've always said, I think this would have been a different story if it had been the police sergeant's daughter,' he said. 'You've got to ask the question, why don't people do their job properly? Why don't they? There are a myriad of reasons, aren't there … indifference, tiredness, poor training, preconception, stereotyping? Charli didn't have much of a record, but she'd been in a bit of trouble. It doesn't take much in a country town for the police to look at you in a negative way.'

The inquest findings did reveal something about what appeared to be one key failing in NSW Police's systems.

Before Charli died, Logan was charged by police in the Australian Capital Territory with assaulting her. He had been released on bail, on the grounds he was not to contact her or be within 100 metres of her without her permission.

Two months later, Logan was arrested again, this time for malicious damage, at his mother's house, where Charli was present. That was just over the border, in New South Wales. The coroner said it was unclear whether NSW Police knew about the bail conditions. There was evidence that the two police forces, whose jurisdictions share a border, have a system that can share a 'block of information' between them, but not the details of individual cases.

The coroner asked for more information about this and got a police statement. For some reason, that statement is completely blacked out in the public report.

In her findings, the coroner said she wanted the New South Wales government to further consider 'whether any failure of systems or services may have contributed to the distress Charli felt in the lead-up to her death'.

If police had known about Logan's bail conditions, would he have been taken into custody earlier, when officers had attended his mother's house? Would the police have been able to protect Charli?

NSW Police declined to be interviewed about Charli's case but did provide a written statement:

The NSW Police Force notes the findings of the Deputy State Coroner in relation to the death of Charli Powell at Queanbeyan in 2019. A comprehensive review of the findings is underway and any recommendations that are directed to police will be considered.

* * *

Sitting in a sunshine-lit armchair at her daughter-in-law's Queanbeyan house, Sharon fought back tears as Kathryn asked why she believed the police response to her teenage daughter's death had been haphazard at best, and a failure at worst.

Her answer was heartbreaking, but all too familiar.

She believed it all came down to the fact her beautiful, bubbly, vivacious daughter was Aboriginal.

'When Charli died, I was out the front,' she said. 'This lady came up to me. I had never actually met her before, but she lived in the house on the corner. She said, "You don't know me, but your beautiful daughter walked past when she was on her way to work in a uniform. She'd be skipping, real happy."

'She asked if I knew something was wrong on Saturday [the day Charli died]. I said, "Well, she called me and asked me to pick her up, but I couldn't get there at the time." She told me she had seen Charli walking around the block. She said she just didn't look like herself. She said she looked so dazed. Like she said she just wasn't her.

'She said, "I want to tell you, Sharon, I've seen Logan chase her down the road ... I've actually rung the police and they've come to my house before."

'Fourteen occasions she had called them, and not once did they knock on my door and say, "Ms Moore, are you aware this is going on with your minor daughter?"

'I can't get my head around it. She was just a kid. She was seventeen. Why did they not help? Was it because she's black?

'I don't know. I still don't know. But it's not right.'

DYING TO BE HEARD

In March 2024, two years after the fateful International Women's Day event that sparked the entire *Dying Rose* investigation, Courtney Hunter-Hebberman attended the *Advertiser*'s Woman of the Year Awards.

In a room full of South Australia's most admirable women, she was named the *Advertiser* Foundation's Inspiration of the Year. It was a full-circle moment for Courtney, whose unwavering bravery in the face of unfathomable grief had touched the lives of so many others – and brought to light a national shame.

Overcome with emotion, Courtney took to the stage. Her opening words were met with raucous applause.

'On behalf of Aboriginal women, we are saying we have had enough,' she told a room of more than two hundred guests. 'We would like all of you to stand with us and push back against this, because it shouldn't be happening today.'

She described the *Dying Rose* project as 'a really, really difficult journey', but one that had given a voice to women who had been silenced.

'This was for Rose, and for all of the women,' she said. 'What we did was bring the voices of our loved ones who have passed away into this world right here, right now.'

She said their voices had resonated across the country.

'The more we speak up and talk about what is happening, the more we can stop it.

'On the eve of International Women's Day in 2022, I was invited to do a Welcome to Country, and I thought, *Oh my God, what am I going to say?* Because sometimes we do a Welcome but we are not actually welcome – and the theme that year was "breaking the bias".'

Back in 2022, she hadn't seen any evidence of bias being broken down – far from it. Not for Aboriginal women.

Now she told the crowd that racism was still embedded in our social institutions today – including the police force and the media, with devastating consequences for Indigenous women and girls.

Courtney held up the award. 'This is to honour my daughter, Rose,' she said. 'For Aboriginal people, we say the spirit is still with us. My daughter is still here in this room – all those women are still here in this room.'

After Courtney returned to her chair, she was approached by a woman who had been sitting just a few seats away: one of the state's most senior authority figures, SA Police's deputy commissioner, Linda Williams.

Dying to be Heard

Ms Williams invited Courtney to a meeting with her and the police commissioner, Grant Stevens, to discuss Courtney's concerns about both the investigation into Rose's death and broader issues it had raised. It was a hand of friendship extended by a representative of the organisation Courtney had, for so long, believed would never listen to her. For the first time, police were going to listen to her, and the most senior police at that.

But Courtney's is only one of the families whose questions we had tried to answer. We'd investigated five others. Each one of these families had been dismissed, left to pick up the pieces of their shattered lives, without the closure that would likely have been afforded to non-Indigenous Australians.

Their stories were confronting. To many Australians, they might even seem unbelievable – because every one of these families had interactions with police that defy belief. But their stories shouldn't be disregarded as unlikely.

For two years, the *Dying Rose* team heard those stories firsthand. We walked the journey of heartache, frustration and despair alongside the families – witnessing the depths of their grief, made even more profound by what they believed were inadequate responses from authorities.

We spoke to six families in total – but their grief and distress are echoed in the lives of the thousands of Aboriginal and Torres Strait Islander people who are abandoned by the nation's justice systems each day.

DYING ROSE

* * *

In October 2021, when auburn-haired four-year-old Cleo Smith disappeared from a campsite in Carnarvon, Western Australia, police were dispatched seven minutes after her distraught family called.

Within forty-eight hours, the Western Australian premier, Mark McGowan, had announced a $1 million reward for information about her disappearance. A taskforce of more than a hundred officers was launched, forensic leads were scoured – and little Cleo was found before it was too late.

This is the response a distraught family deserves in a time of unimaginable panic.

This was not the response afforded to ten-month-old Indigenous boy Charlie Mullaley, also abducted in Western Australia.

In 2013, Charlie's mother, Tamica, was beaten to within an inch of her life by her then partner and left naked and bleeding in the street. When police arrived at the scene, their attention was turned not to her abuser, but to Tamica herself, who was badly injured and grew agitated when her father, Ted Mullaley, arrived and they wouldn't let her leave with him.

She was handcuffed by police, thrown into a paddy wagon and taken away – to hospital rather than the police station, at Ted's insistence. They left Charlie behind with others at the scene, despite Ted's request that they take him too. The

Dying to be Heard

man who had beaten Tamica later returned and took Charlie, saying he would take him to family. When Ted found out, he pleaded repeatedly with police to launch an immediate search, saying that Tamica's partner had previously made threats to harm the baby, but police took hours to act. Even then, there was no taskforce. There was no search. They only issued licence plate details for the car the man was driving.

Charlie was subjected to fifteen hours of torture, receiving injuries to almost every inch of his tiny body before he died the next day. Tamica was charged with assaulting police and Ted with obstructing police.

Years later, the Western Australian government would pardon Tamica and her father and issue a formal apology. The Western Australian attorney-general told Charlie's family, 'I am sorry for the way you were treated by the government and the WA Police, both before and after losing baby Charlie.'

But that is cold comfort for Charlie's family, who lost their little boy because they weren't listened to when they most urgently needed to be heard.

Most Australians know Cleo Smith's name, and her story. Very few know Charlie Mullaley's. A deep racial divide is evident not just in the experiences of Indigenous and non-Indigenous Australians in dealing with the police, but also in the level of public and media interest in their stories.

The stories we've examined in this book make that clear, and Lasonya Dutton's case is perhaps the best example. Keith

DYING ROSE

Dutton told Douglas that if his daughter had been white, police and the media would have been 'all over it like a rash', which seems likely: if a young white woman, a mother of two children, living in a well-to-do suburb in a capital city, were mysteriously found dead in the backyard of her family home, her decomposing corpse being gnawed at by animals, her death would surely be the focus of a major investigation, and the media coverage would go on for weeks, even months – but in Lasonya Dutton's case, no one seemed to care.

* * *

In the chapter telling Rose Hunter-Hebberman's story, we noted that suicide is the leading cause of death for young people in Australia, and that the suicide rate is significantly higher among young First Nations people than their non-Indigenous counterparts. For that reason, it's not surprising that suicide is one of the first explanations police consider when confronted with the unexpected death of a young First Nations woman.

But there are other disturbing statistics that police should also be taking into account. While the suicide rate for First Nations women is around 2.5 times that of non-Indigenous women, their murder rate is on average around eight or nine times higher. It is higher still for First Nations women living in remote communities. That means any investigation into the unexpected death of a young First Nations woman should at least consider the possibility that she was a victim of others' violence until it can be ruled out.

Former homicide detective Gary Jubelin agrees. He told Douglas that making assumptions was one of the biggest mistakes a detective investigating a death can make. 'You can't find a body at the bottom of a cliff and say, "Oh, it must be suicide," or find someone hanging and say, "It must be suicide." What I was taught by the people that trained me, my mentors, and what I passed on is that every suspicious death ... should be treated as a homicide until it can be proven otherwise.'

You might have heard the term 'Closing the Gap'. It originated from calls for governments to 'close up' the unacceptable gap between health outcomes and life expectancy for Indigenous and non-Indigenous Australians, which is now an official target of the National Agreement on Closing the Gap. Another of the agreement's targets, less often reported on, is to reduce the rate of all forms of family violence and abuse against Indigenous women and children by at least 50 per cent by 2031. But to fix the problem, we first have to understand why it's happening – and to understand, we need to listen to those with lived experience.

That is why, in October 2021 – only a few weeks after Charlene Warrior was found hanging from a tree in Bute – Senator Dorinda Cox, a Yamatji–Noongar woman and former police officer, used her maiden speech to parliament to call for a senate inquiry into missing and murdered Aboriginal women and children.

'In my jurisdiction, police are able to mount a taskforce in days for missing women and children,' Senator Cox would later explain. 'They will mobilise hundreds of officers, send up drones and triangulate phones. But for a black woman in this country, they cannot do that. And I want to know why. Time is of the essence in these cases. But we see cases where a child is dead because someone failed to understand the urgency of that case ... Where's the outcry? Where's the justice?'

At the same time *Dying Rose* was being produced, the inquiry Senator Cox had called for was under way in the Australian Parliament. It had called for submissions and begun conducting hearings in 2022.

The first 'term of reference' or objective of the missing and murdered First Nations women and children inquiry was to find out exactly how many missing and murdered women and children there were. The simple answer is: too many. A more complex question is why authorities don't know exactly how many First Nations women and children have either been murdered or gone missing in recent years.

The inquiry also set out to examine current and historical institutional responses to all forms of violence experienced by First Nations women and children, including the practices followed and resources expended when investigating deaths and missing person reports.

At the end of the inquiry's terms of reference is a sad question about how these women and children can be commemorated.

There were clear parallels between the questions senate committee members were asking in the national capital and the questions the *Dying Rose* team was confronting in Adelaide, so we watched the inquiry's progress with interest. Due to the sensitive nature of the evidence provided, many of the submissions from families who had experienced the death or disappearance of a loved one were made confidentially, but there were also several public hearings, at different locations across the country – and in 2023, we travelled to Gadigal land to be present as those at the coalface of the issue were interviewed by the committee in a ritzy hotel in the Sydney CBD.

There were no more than twenty chairs laid out for the media and families, indicating the level of interest the organisers had anticipated, and about ten people sitting in them. Only four were other journalists. It was disappointing, given the gravity of the subject to be discussed.

Christine Robinson from the Wirringa Baiya Aboriginal Women's Legal Centre and Dixie Link-Gordon from the Aboriginal Women's Advisory Network appeared that day and told harrowing stories, from their clients' experiences and their own, of how issues within the police force negatively influence its response to First Nations people.

Their words echoed those of Courtney Hunter-Hebberman early in our investigation, when she said that racism can be invisible to Australians who haven't experienced it. First Nations people can see it and feel it, rippling through their interactions with an institution that is supposed to protect them from harm.

'As Aboriginal women, we understand the subtle racism and discrimination. And I don't think other people, like non-Aboriginal people, understand it to our level,' Ms Robinson said. 'I look at some of those cases sometimes, and I think you can see the discrimination, you can see the racism, you can see those different kinds of behaviours or those attitudes. But it's not always recognised by the non-Aboriginal people around the table, because they've never been scrutinised or never been under that microscope of being an Aboriginal person to understand what that looks like.'

Ms Robinson said workers at the Aboriginal Women's Legal Centre often found that there were poor response times from police when it came to crisis calls from Indigenous women – or no response at all – particularly in regional areas such as Bute. 'Sometimes, in some of the communities, they call for assistance from police that arrives twenty-four hours later,' she said.

But when police do respond, as we've seen, their response can be inappropriate, inadequate and, in the worst cases, traumatising – like when police arrested Shanarra Bright Campbell's crying brother and dragged him from the house,

Dying to be Heard

rather than doing what they could to help the paramedics desperately trying to save his sister's life.

* * *

Over the past two years, the *Dying Rose* team had lost count of the times we had tried to get different police forces to talk to us – in South Australia, the Northern Territory and New South Wales. None of them would answer questions directly, nor would they sit down for an interview – only issuing statements through their media teams.

At 9.45 am on the morning of the senate inquiry hearing in Sydney, three senior officers from NSW Police walked in and took their places in front of the panel. This was the first time the team had had the opportunity to see police respond in person to questions about systemic issues affecting the treatment of Indigenous women and children.

Behind the microphones were NSW Police Superintendent Christopher Nicholson; head of the Homicide Squad, Detective Superintendent Danny Doherty; and Detective Inspector Ritchie Sim, manager of the Missing Persons Registry.

Superintendent Nicholson opened by speaking about NSW Police's cultural awareness programs and Indigenous engagement. Whatever the senators asked, the police commanders kept coming back to these things – cultural awareness programs and Indigenous engagement. Asked what

NSW Police had done to tackle racial bias in the wake of the high-profile Bowraville murders case, discussed earlier in this book, they gave the same answer again – cultural awareness programs and Indigenous engagement.

But when the questions moved on to how many Indigenous police officers there were in the police force, things began to get heated.

Det Supt Doherty was asked to name one Aboriginal female employee in his charge. He could not.

Greens Senator David Shoebridge then posed the question: 'If you think people have difficulty identifying as Aboriginal and Torres Strait Islander in the police, do you think some of that might be a NSW Police problem?'

But the officers were adamant it was not. 'No, that's a personal choice,' Supt Nicholson said.

Senator Cox asked the three police commanders, point blank, whether they accepted there was racism in the policing institution.

Again, Supt Nicholson denied that racism was a systemic issue in the New South Wales police force. 'The commissioner expects that all police will act with respect to all people, whether in custody or victims,' he said. 'So that kind of behaviour is not only not condoned anymore, but we encourage all police to speak up against that behaviour. When they do, we've got strong, robust governance that makes sure we investigate it appropriately.'

He proposed that any racism within the police force was a matter of dealing with 'a few bad eggs'. That was also the position of senior members of the NT Police, of course, before Zachary Rolfe's evidence at the coronial inquest into the death of Kumanjayi Walker exposed just how widespread, and how overt, racist attitudes were among his former colleagues.

Entrenched bias within the policing system is a subject Senator Cox has a particular interest in, having experienced it firsthand. She told the inquiry that her cousin's death had been ruled to be manslaughter after police decided that her own history of violence had been a factor in her violent end.

'Police justified not investigating her case to the point where the offender was then found guilty of manslaughter, not murder,' she said. 'There was a decision at the core of that that was not the same as if it was a non-Indigenous woman, because of her history or because of her postcode.'

She said police often responded to Indigenous women differently than they would to non-Indigenous women, but that they denied this was an issue of race, saying they made decisions on a case-by-case basis, taking into account their prior knowledge of or interactions with an individual woman.

The senator felt strongly that a woman's history should be irrelevant: the police response should always be to prioritise her safety, regardless of their past interactions with her. The mother of seventeen-year-old 'troublemaker' Charli Powell would no doubt agree.

DYING ROSE

Later that day, knowing it might be our only chance to speak to police face to face in the course of our investigation, the *Dying Rose* team waited on the bustling footpath outside the hotel where the senate inquiry was held, hoping to speak to the three police officers on their way out. After more than twenty minutes, Supt Nicholson finally appeared – and we finally had the opportunity to ask about the issues investigated in the podcast.

Emily put a question to him. 'One of the things that you didn't touch on in there is cases that have been ruled suicide upon arrival,' she said, explaining that families sometimes felt that other possibilities were overlooked – for example, where a woman's partner had a history of violence. 'Is there a mechanism for families to say, "No, there's a history of violence, and we want this looked into?"' she asked.

'We continue to improve the cultural awareness, training and education of our police,' Supt Nicholson said. 'We want to ensure that we are listening to our Aboriginal communities.' He said that NSW Police saw its Aboriginal employees as 'guiding the way' in how police were trained and how they communicated with Aboriginal communities. 'And we will continue to do that and will continue to learn as we go on,' Supt Nicholson said.

Emily pushed a little harder: 'A lot of these families believe that history coloured their interactions with police. They believe that police arrived and said, as Senator Cox said inside the inquiry, "This is a troublemaker, it's a bit of a hard basket, we don't want to look further into this." Is it acceptable that police might be introducing biases based on previous interactions, and what is being done to tackle that?'

'We recognise the injustices of the past,' Supt Nicholson told her. 'We said that in our opening statement inside. And so the training, the cultural immersion, our engagement with the community is all about learning from our Aboriginal communities on the best way to engage Aboriginal communities as we go forward.'

To his credit, Supt Nicholson was the first police representative prepared to answer our questions – but that was little comfort to the families of the women whose deaths we had been investigating.

* * *

The senate inquiry's intention was to bring about genuine change, but Australia first needs to acknowledge the necessity of that change – which means confronting our past, and considering how it has shaped the present.

Khatija Thomas is a Kokatha woman and a lawyer with the Aboriginal Legal Rights Movement, an organisation that provides legal representation to First Nations people. It was representatives of the ALRM who petitioned the South

Australian coroner, without success, to hold an inquest into Charlene Warrior's death.

Ms Thomas told the inquiry that Aboriginal victims of family violence were often traumatised and retraumatised by their interactions with police. To understand why, it is important to understand that First Nations people have a long, complex relationship with police that stretches all the way back to colonisation.

'The use of the police in moving Aboriginal people off their land was key to legitimising the state's dispossession of Aboriginal people,' Ms Thomas said. 'Aboriginal people didn't have a home to go to. We didn't have food or water. The government was forcing us to have rations of just tea and sugar and flour. That was what we were given to eat, because we weren't able to access our own land anymore to feed ourselves in our traditional ways.'

She said the police had been on the frontline as Aboriginal people were pushed off their land, to the 'outsides and edges of society'. It was a legacy that continued on. Ms Thomas said Australians had inherited a police force that was essentially an arm of government, used from the very beginning to control Aboriginal people – and as policing grew into an institution, the attitudes and approaches to Aboriginal people of those early days had remained. 'They just find a new way of manifesting or being put into action in the contemporary context,' she said.

To say Australia's policing system is 'racist' is not a reflection on any individual officer, Ms Thomas said. It's about the system itself, and how the culture of an institution responds to Aboriginal people.

She said a lot of these issues were easily dismissed as 'just bad individual experiences', but when looked at through an Aboriginal lens, the overarching narrative is one of mistrust and not being taken seriously – which tells us this is a systemic issue.

'It's not that one officer is racist, necessarily, but the entire system behind them is built off racism. There are a lot of good individuals trying to do good things, and we find allies often, but unfortunately, not often enough.'

Racist bias isn't always active, or even conscious, as we discussed earlier. It manifests in many other ways – as systemic disadvantage, for example, and through cultural misunderstanding.

For First Nations people dealing with grief and loss, their experience is worsened by a system that is challenging for all – including non-Aboriginal people – to navigate.

'Non-Aboriginal people have different ways of understanding how to navigate systems because they have grown up in them,' Ms Thomas said. 'Even keeping certain types of paperwork, or a filing cabinet. A lot of Aboriginal people wouldn't document or write down things because we come from an oral tradition.

'The weight that the law puts on things like written evidence, compared to the way an Aboriginal person would put a story forward, is one of those systemic biases that disadvantages us from being taken seriously.'

Reluctance to acknowledge racism often stems from fear of individual blame or a desperate avoidance of guilt – or, in some instances, racism may be so deeply entrenched that it seems justified to those perpetrating it, Ms Thomas says.

But to understand how racism manifests itself within a structure or system, or how it becomes accepted within the culture of an organisation, we first must acknowledge that it exists.

'We all stand on the shoulders of those who have come before us, whether it's in a good way or in a negative way,' Ms Thomas said.

'There are a lot of individual, really good police officers out there and there are a lot of really good men out there as well ... it's not about being anti any individuals, it's actually about how the systems and the culture of those institutions respond to Aboriginal people.'

Leading Indigenous voices say our systems are failing First Nations Australians because they have not been created with them at heart.

'We have to be able to tackle racism at its core. We have to be able to unpack it and to really understand how it manifests itself within a structure or a system, and how it's accepted within that culture of that organisation,' Senator Cox said.

'Systemic racism becomes practice that's passed down from senior officers to very junior officers straight out of the police academy, because they might tell junior officers: "We don't follow that policy," or "We don't do it like that." It may not be as obvious as saying it, but that's the covert racism that happens.'

Rose's mother Courtney said she believed racial bias was embedded within the investigative processes – creating tension from the first point of contact with Aboriginal communities.

'We can't trust the police to do the investigations and actually have an outcome,' she said. 'It puts fear into you, it makes you feel like you're not being listened to – it invalidates you. It's gaslighting. The state is telling you that what you're feeling isn't right, or what you're seeing and what you're hearing isn't right.'

* * *

Over two years, the *Dying Rose* podcast team approached authorities more than a dozen times, searching for a response to the deaths of six women whose families felt their questions had gone unheard. Not one representative agreed to an interview.

That wall of silence speaks to the challenges grieving families face when seeking justice for the loss of someone they love.

DYING ROSE

Indigenous leader Nyunggai Warren Mundine has spoken on this issue publicly, stressing how important it is for police to be open in their communication, especially with frightened or grieving families.

'There's a compassionate way of dealing with these things,' he said. 'Sitting down and having conversations with people – that's how they should be operating. Police should be ... sitting down and having that conversation with the family. Because any death, under any circumstances, is a tragic thing for a family.'

Mr Mundine said better systems should be put in place to facilitate those conversations. 'If the families are feeling let down and not supported then I think those things could be discussed and worked on,' he said.

His comments certainly resonate when you think of Sue Nowland's long correspondence with the detective handling her daughter Lyla Nettle's case. Many of Sue's questions could have been addressed far more quickly and effectively in a short phone call or face-to-face conversation, but instead, due to long response times, simple misunderstandings dragged on for months or were never cleared up at all. The process seemed calculated to aggravate Sue's concerns rather than assuage them.

Mr Mundine noted that lines of communication between Aboriginal communities and police had improved in recent decades, but that there was further progress to be made – and a key part of building trust and improving the relationship was recruitment of more Aboriginal police officers.

'It's a historical thing, in regard to police and the Aboriginal community, because police were the ones who had to enforce all the old discriminatory legislation and laws,' he said. 'But in the last probably thirty years there's been a big turnaround in that with the police reaching out and wanting to work with Aboriginal communities.

'We do need a situation where Aboriginal people can feel comfortable with police and that when they need help they can feel comfortable picking up that phone and talking to the police about it.'

Again, this resonates with the stories of the women in this book. When Charlene Warrior's sister Theresa spoke with the Aboriginal grieving officer at Port Augusta, she said it was the first time in her dealings with the police that she felt heard or believed. Similarly, Douglas noted the hope Keith Dutton felt when he first received a call from the newly appointed Aboriginal support officer at the New South Wales coroner's court, and the relief the family felt after her visit to Wilcannia, convinced that at last someone had understood and was listening to them.

That's why recruiting Aboriginal police officers is so important. For the Aboriginal community, seeing people in uniform who share their lived experience and cultural understanding goes a long way towards breaking down the 'us and them' nature of their relationship with the police.

* * *

At times, it has been difficult for Douglas to come to terms with what he has to cover as Indigenous Affairs reporter, including *Dying Rose* and the debate around the 2023 Voice referendum. In the weeks after the referendum dramatically failed, Douglas wrestled with continuing a column advocating for Aboriginal people – but ploughed on with reporting after seeing the power of the *Dying Rose* investigation.

'As Aboriginal people we are natural storytellers,' Douglas says, 'but too often our stories are not taken seriously or believed. They're just, you know, yarns.' The value of the project for him was in helping grieving families find the widest possible audience for their stories.

A fundamental principle the team was guided by was to let the families speak for themselves. We wanted to promote Aboriginal voices, and particularly Aboriginal women's voices – that's one reason that we chose to produce a podcast, rather than limiting our reporting to print and online channels.

Right from the outset, Gemma thought that would give the stories the greatest impact. 'If you're going to bring to life a story like this and give people who struggle to be heard a voice, then what better way than hearing it in their own words, actually hearing their voices?' she said.

We also wanted to centre the voices of the families – not those of authorities or academics – acknowledging them as the experts on their own lives.

One of the few academics we did consult was Margaret Castles, a senior law lecturer at the University of Adelaide – who just happened to be the best friend of Mandy Brown, Rose Hunter-Hebberman's grandmother, and also Emily's former lecturer. With her legal expertise and personal connection to Rose, Marg was uniquely poised to observe how interactions with authorities had taken their toll on the family and to put their experiences into a broader context for us.

'I deal with lots of people who encounter these barriers over and over and over again,' she said. 'For them, it feels like every time they want to open their mouth and say something, every time they think, *I want to be heard, and I want justice*, it's a battle. Women – and in particular Aboriginal women – are not taken seriously. Then, when the worst happens, the family is also voiceless. It's almost like the individual never has a voice and is silenced throughout the whole process.'

Marg said families, particularly First Nations families and those facing socioeconomic disadvantage, were often met with a brick wall if they questioned authorities' responses.

'One of the things that I think is a real problem is that when people start asking questions, authorities tend to close down and become defensive and push back,' she said. 'Even if it is a suicide, there's a big story behind the suicide. The problem is that respectful responses from authorities would tell that story – but the law is not interested in people's stories. That, I think, is an enormous failing – particularly when you're dealing with humans, human lives and human deaths.'

When people say Indigenous women have no voice, they are wrong. Indigenous women are out there every day, advocating for themselves and their families and community, speaking as loudly as they can. The problem is that not enough people are listening.

When the senate report into murdered and missing First Nations women and children was released in August 2024, Senator Dorinda Cox was deeply disappointed. She said she felt 'immense love and respect' for all of the people who had spoken to the committee, but that the report's ten recommendations didn't go far enough.

'Much has been written about the harrowing nature of the stories heard during the inquiry,' she said, 'and it's important that we hear about the suffering. It's our job to stop the suffering. But it won't happen until we get frontline government services to care, and sometimes the message that we get is some people don't care.'

* * *

Dying to be Heard

The *Dying Rose* investigation started by asking questions about one young woman's unexpected death. Ultimately, it uncovered a national shame: the often callous indifference of authorities to the deaths of Indigenous women and girls, and the appalling treatment received by their families. Sadly, it also revealed an almost complete apathy in the wider public when Aboriginal women and girls are missing or die suddenly.

But there is hope.

Courtney Hunter-Hebberman was pleased by the response when Rose's episode of the podcast was first released. She said she felt like someone had actually listened to her.

It was millions of people, in fact. Millions have read stories associated with the podcast and more have listened to the podcast episodes around the world. There are people out there who care – people who want to know more, who want to understand.

There is still significantly more work to do for Indigenous Australians. First Nations women's deaths are not talked about enough and not reported on enough.

Speaking to these families, the depths of grief that they feel and the layers of injustice that they faced, it's almost impossible to not hear that something needs to change.

The *Dying Rose* team listened to these stories for two years – and listened to a system that was failing people, over and over and over again.

DYING ROSE

There is no panacea, but we can look at our institutional machines and the outcomes they are producing and decide that enough is enough.

All six of the families we spoke to could have been afforded more compassion and respect.

To witness their bravery and willingness to trust us with their stories, particularly in situations where they had shared their experiences with police and didn't feel they had been listened to, was nothing short of extraordinary.

The worst thing any parent could fathom is to lose a child. But to then tell that story in the desperate hope of change requires unimaginable courage.

These families' stories are finally being shared – but are not easy to hear. It is too late to save Rose, Charlene, Lasonya, Lyla, Shanarra and Charli.

But to save the lives of other Aboriginal women and children, we now have to listen.

ACKNOWLEDGEMENTS

The authors thank the families of the women who appear in these pages for opening their hearts and lives and sharing their sorrows so their daughters' stories could be told.

The *Dying Rose* investigation has grown from a small gathering in the Adelaide Hills to a cross-country mission to tell the stories of Rose, Charlene, Lasonya, Lyla, Shanarra and Charli. The reporting team would like to thank News Corp's editorial director of audio, Dan Box, audio producer Jasper Leak and group editorial legal counsel Stephen Coombs, without whom the investigation would not have been possible.

We would also like to extend our thanks to Mary Rennie and the team at HarperCollins for commissioning this book and for all of their encouragement.

This is a story about First Nations women. The team who put this work together also pay their respects to First Nations women and children.

295